JOURNEY INTO
Love

JOURNEY INTO

Love

From Fear
to Freedom

NAN C. MERRILL

continuum

NEW YORK • LONDON

2007

The Continuum International Publishing Group Inc
80 Maiden Lane, New York, NY 10038

The Continuum International Publishing Group Ltd
The Tower Building, 11 York Road, London SE1 7NX

www.continuumbooks.com

Printed in Canada on 100% postconsumer
waste recycled paper.

 green
press
INITIATIVE

Library of Congress Cataloging-in-Publication Data

Merrill, Nan C.
  Journey into love : from fear to freedom / Nan C. Merrill.
    p.   cm.
  ISBN-13: 978-0-8264-1904-0 (pbk. : alk. paper)
  ISBN-10: 0-8264-1904-6 (pbk. : alk. paper)   1. Jesus Christ—Biography.
  I. Title.

  BT301.9.M47   2007
  232.9'5—dc22

                                                        2007033199

Every reasonable effort has been made to locate the owners of rights to
previously published works in this book. Grateful acknowledgment is made to
Father Matthew Kelly for permission to quote from *Flute Solo*.

Contents

Part I

Journey into Love

From Fear to Freedom

Preface

Journey into Love invites us to celebrate the wondrous shining light each of us is meant to radiate and to discover, uncover, and recognize the ego-fear illusions that distract us from our birthright—the peace of God. For, we are born to live joyously, to express our unique Beingness freely as co-creators with the Beloved. As each wave of the ocean is integral to the whole ocean, so each of our lives is an integral page of the Big Story, the great Cosmic Mystery.

Once we learn that our fears are but illusions of the big lie, the great myth of our "sinfulness" and "guilt," once we recognize that our fear-defenses have been unconsciously formed from cradle and, regrettably for many, to crypt, we awaken, freer now to follow the route of forgiveness, love, and at-one-ment that Jesus so powerfully lived and taught. As we journey together along these roads, we may come to live into the resurrection experience of Oneness, Unity with All That Is. Then, while we still live in this dream world where nightmares seem real, we are no longer of it; rather, we are One with Reality and, therefore, we extend it out to those who yearn for Home. One might say that we move from hell to heaven . . . from fear to expressions of love, freedom, and deep inner joy that radiates out to others around the world. Simple, yet ever so elusive without guidelines and surrender.

No matter how difficult, unfulfilled, frustrated, or unworthy we may feel our lives have been or seem to be, *everything* and *everyone* have been and continue to be our teacher, one way or another, in this dream world of time. Yet as we Awaken in the moments of forgiveness, the dream-illusion disappears. Recall the two beggars beside Jesus on their crosses. One Awakened in recognizing Who Jesus is; he knew forgiveness and Love, while the other languished and seemed to die alone. Blessed companions on the journey, *we are never alone!* To recognize and acknowledge the living, loving, and guiding Divine Companion with and within us is a key to walking the various roads that we are invited to travel on the way to authentic living, to deep peace, and gentle joy. Jesus, awakened to Christ Consciousness, is our guide *par excellence*, ever ready to welcome us Home.

In preparation for this soul-journey, we will first discover and reclaim the strength and power of our own names and ponder expanded ways to experience baptism. In all probability, we will begin this process carrying too much old baggage. Yet, as we face our inner demons in and through the wilderness roads and as our fears diminish, we find ourselves freer to travel with far less to carry. Simplicity, times of solitude, deep inner silence, abiding peace, assurance, gratitude, and gentle inner joy will become some of our companioning friends.

As we grow in openness and receptivity, we are ready to meet our neighbor on the road to Jericho. Here we face our wounded-ness, our masks and persona—the ways we are seen by others. We discover the habits, beliefs, and thought patterns in our lives that override and diminish our compassion-quotient and all that keeps us from experiencing and expressing our life-giving potential. With forgiveness as a key to unlock our fears and projections on to others, we become freer to let go of what may be, in reality, "yesterday's will of God;"[1] we rediscover and recover the Divine Child, who, sadly for many of us, has been neglected, held hostage, or—even now—remains unknown. Liberated, we can respond more spontaneously and naturally to the present moment with surprise and wonder.

The road to Jerusalem cannot be bypassed. For to meet Love deeply within our hearts, we must be empty, willing to face our deep fears of death, nothingness, and abandonment. Yet, paradoxically, abandonment into the Hands of Love is the very act that leads us to the trust and faith we need to let go of all that keeps us from true fulfillment and deep compassion. Knowing that we are surrendering ourselves into Good Hands is not always much consolation, as Jesus found out at Gethsemene, the road to the Cross. And for those of us who had difficult relationships, especially with authority figures in our childhood, we may find that gentle, loving wisdom figures such as Sophia or Mary may be more resonant within our hearts. As in the wilderness roads, we are left alone to pray, to listen in the Silence, and, eventually—if and as we face our fears—to discover our false ego-selves becoming transformed. When we look in the mirror we may be humbled to see a more mature, authentic presence yearning to follow the path of service, love, and joy. Then we are free to walk the Emmaus road with praise, gratitude, and thanksgiving . . . to join in the Great Dance of life with all those who have taken or are now embarking consciously on the Journey.

Even so, the path does not end here; for, another road awaits us. On the road to Galilee, we are led by the Spirit of Truth, our angels, and guides. And though we may be asked to serve in places we would rather not go, we now *know* that we are not alone. Christ's Loving Companion Presence is so imprinted upon our hearts that we are filled with joy so that, even without words, we begin to radiate *LoveConsciousness*[2] to whomever we meet, wherever we are.

While this is a simple outline of Jesus' pilgrimage to show us how to live in Love's Light and Power, it isn't a one, two, three process. Each of the roads is presented as we are ready in our everyday lives, several of them simultaneously much of the time. Though I have questioned Jesus' promise that we will never be given more than we can bear, in truth I have always grown from the difficult times and, in retrospect, often much later, I have given thanks with heartfelt gratitude for the new life garnered from the experiences. We can face the challenges with far more grace and courage as we become ever more conscious of our own unique path. To know we are never truly alone, to cooperate with our many unseen guides while committing ourselves to the Process can turn our journeys into the most life-giving, wondrous adventure imaginable.

To share my spiritual Awakening and soul journey authentically with you, dear companions, has taken over thirty years. Facing and overcoming a lingering fear of being seen as "different, not quite all right," on the one hand, and wrestling with the possibility of shadow temptations/ego-illusions creeping in, on the other hand, as well as new Awakenings over the years has been both a maturing process and deeper journey into Love. This book has emerged in response to individuals I have met at various retreats and gatherings or from those I have counseled along the way. One man, who was making his first retreat, rather shyly, and yet with great emotion, shared his new insights:

"I am forty-five years old and have attended church most of my life. I never knew until now that we—all of us—are on a journey. It never occurred to me that following Jesus meant anything more than doing good and going to church. I never saw Jesus' Story as my story. I feel as if I now have one foot on the road—and, even though it seems late, I am excited. I am also afraid that I will not get very far without someone to walk a ways with me, someone to help me feel more comfortable with Jesus by my side."

Then, when a number of others wrote that the sharing of my journey stories had helped them get in touch with their own walk in faith, I began to write. More and more, I have come to recognize that while Scripture, religions, and theology may act as catalysts for our spiritual maturing, and may facilitate deeper understanding *about* the Source of our Being, we are profoundly blessed as we *consciously* choose to live into the guidelines of Jesus' "Love Story" given as gift to us. The Door is ever open and an invitation is extended to all to enter into Awakening on our pilgrimage soul journey to healing, wholeness, holiness, and Love. Each of our experiences on the roads will be in our own perfect timing and readiness. For some, it is a life time odyssey, while many gently choose to follow step by step, and still others, like Jesus or Paul, are thrust into the journey whether they feel ready or not. We are called to action, to choose or to wrestle on this pilgrimage; one way or another, we make our life's journey in our own unique way.

However we come to Awaken, we are never alone. We have the Source of our being, Jesus, the Holy Spirit, guides, angels and our own higher Self to guide us all along the way. Ask and the Door to heightened awareness will be opened as we learn to listen deeply in the Silence. Love's gentle Voice will be heard. We are eternally united as One in this Story and we bless one another with every step we take along the way.

Over many decades I have come to *know* that fear is our inner "enemy"; fear separates us from Love. As we acknowledge our ego-fear illusions and are willing to face them one by one, as we recognize and transform their distracting, debilitating energy forgiving all that has been a part of their development, we find a profound love and a deep trust awakening in their place. Truly, with the guidance and wholeness of Love, our inner guides, and the angelic realm in this journey, our fears will no longer enslave us.

I take full responsibility for the many "liberties" that I have taken in sharing the roads that Jesus walked as well as the words I created for emphasis or clarity, and my witnessing to some of the dire concerns in today's world, as well as a bit of "theological" re-visioning. I share these stories and meditations out of lived experience as illustrations; I hope they may serve as catalysts for your own unique pilgrimage into Love.

Each of us walks this journey uniquely. As we face the mystery and wonder of our own lives, we may discover other spirit-filled roads on the path to Awakening. I wish each of you, dear companions, myriad and heartfelt blessings on this pilgrimage that we call life!

Introduction

$\mathcal{W}$hen it was that She made herself known to me once again, I cannot recall. Surely, She was with me at birth. Yet the culture, centuries of unacknowledged imbalance of energies—masculine ruling over feminine—soon conspired to veil her Presence. For, inexorably, as She living in me began to threaten patriarchal authority, She was shunted away like a skeleton in a basement closet, like a prisoner in a solitary cell—ignored, unnamed, debased when seen, and rendered invisible. No blame here . . . such is the way it was. Still, it mattered to me; it matters more profoundly as I am aware of the wounding that continues to fester and spread dis-ease each time She is not allowed to participate fully in the Divine Dance we call Life. So, I am compelled to find my voice, Her Voice in me, and speak it.

I write as a laywoman who loves the Mystery, the Beloved, the Divine in All . . . a woman who has known the burden of fear and pain and who has experienced the heights of love and joy, thanks to the wise counsel and loving support of many, many individuals along the way. I write as an enthusiastic seeker who is grateful for intuitions of profound, world-shaking Spiritquakes, which will give rise to a great Awakening of consciousness that seems immanent around the globe, notwithstanding outward events and appearances. I write as a sojourner who prays for forgiveness over the rampant injustice, oppression, and destructive masculine energies that seem to be ravaging cities and nations, as well as Earth Herself. I write in order to share with others what seems to be shouting out to me throughout the New Testament: we are One with the Divine Beloved who is calling us home to live as co-creators in the world, yet not of it . . . to live as beams of light shining in this illusionary world of ego-fear and guilt . . . to *know* that we are Love, which blesses the world as we extend It out to others.

I remember years ago being profoundly moved as I cried my way through the movie *Yentil* several times. Facing many patriarchal obstacles, she embarked on a deep study of the Torah in her passion to know God. The movie stimulated my own deep spiritual yearning to discover how Jesus' teachings, if really lived out, would impact my life. For Scripture was a source of inspiration and guidance since childhood, notwithstanding an inner need to re-vision so much of the patriarchal language and imbalance.

Over the years I have been blessed to study with many other teachers and spiritual modalities. I studied the insights of Carl Jung, which will be readily noted in this journey into Love. However, I must be clear: though I find Jungian terms add clarity, I am not an analyst; I simply find his insights resonant with Jesus' teachings. I pray they might speak to your heart as well.

For years, the discord within my soul forced me to learn survival skills in order to break away from masculine dominance, whether that of authoritarian men or that of women driven by the negative *animus* (inner overpowering masculine energy). It became natural, yet always frustrating and with some resentment, to translate decidedly exclusive masculine language, to dream beyond destructive, competitive, hierarchical, institutional systems to what could be, and to re-vision the incredibly new story that Jesus' life in the world described . . . the story whose depths have yet to be fully plumbed . . . the story that has surely wounded and divided as much as it has healed.

Journey into Love is one answer to my yearning to be in solidarity with the awakening feminine consciousness as it continues at an accelerated pace to be integrated in men and women, birthing a balanced new world where seeds of peace, justice, and creativity will begin to flower.

The overview that follows is given as a backdrop to our journey into love to emphasize how revolutionary Jesus' life and teachings were two thousand years ago, especially in the equality with which he interacts with all people. But we can see how far we have yet to journey in order to live his life lessons more fully in our day. Many years ago, a dear friend and minister asked me what I most hoped to become. I responded, "a good Christian." His reply surprised me. "Wonderful! I'm not sure I've ever met one." That, too, became an impetus to my own journey into Love.

The Good News begins in Matthew's and later in Luke's gospel with the genealogy of Jesus by naming the *fathers* who led up to His birth: a reminder to the reader that the focus of the times is masculine. Mothers and daughters are unnamed and insignificant except to delineate which wife gave birth. Luke's gospel starts with an angel's promise of a child to be born to an elderly, barren couple, Zechariah and Elizabeth. Right away, feminine energy is evoked when the angel, Gabriel, silences Zechariah for nine months for not believing (for being so rational, a masculine quality which is certainly necessary and useful in other circumstances), and thrusting him into a more contemplative mode in preparation for this special birth. He, it seems, is to be pregnant in a different way.

Another change in consciousness is seen when Elizabeth, a *woman*, named their child, John, in the assembly . . . *and*, Zechariah supported her. Afterwards when Zechariah could talk again, his words flowed eloquently through the Holy Spirit—one of the fruits of spending time in the Silence, of being in harmony with the Feminine.

Yet, Elizabeth's response to conception had been to hide herself for five months "to take away my reproach among men." To give birth to one or more *sons* was considered a woman's most fulfilling function. Being barren up to this point, Elizabeth had been seen as a failure; she felt the "failure" keenly. It would have been rare for a woman to question her own identity; to do so would have brought instant retribution.

I am no expert on the structure of drama. Yet, it does seem clear to me that our [Story's] theme (after the litany of genealogy) seems to be the beginning of the Feminine breaking through in everyday life. The major and minor "characters" that move us toward the Good News of Jesus, carry the feminine energy. The old dispensation is threatened and opposes it. Even Zechariah's eloquent prophecy can be seen at one level in the light of a feminine awakening in balance with the masculine. He proclaims that John is to prepare the way for Jesus who

(a.) will "give knowledge of salvation": the balancing of masculine/feminine energies, the undoing of ego-shadows and illusions within—the fears, ignorance, doubts, as well as the gifts and talents that have been unexamined and projected on to others;

(b.) will, "through the forgiveness of sins," bring reconciliation: a recognition of the ego-guilt within us as the dream-illusions that we have created; with forgiveness, peace will replace all illusionary thoughts of conflict;

(c.) will "through the tender mercy of God": teach us of Love's ever present mercy and compassion so that we, too, can learn to become merciful and compassionate, radiating love in the world;

(d.) "when the day shall dawn upon us from on high": masculine and feminine energies will unite, become more balanced and harmonious; that day is emerging *now*, a new dawn;

(e.) will "give light to those who sit in darkness and the shadow of death": light to that which lives unacknowledged in darkness within us that can move us toward uniting the opposites and toward individuation; then, more and more, we become beneficial presences in the world extending love and light and life to others;

(f.) will "guide our feet into the way of peace": as we are in harmony with all of humanity, we *can* live in peace. Jesus modeled the way teaching the disciples, the men and women he called friend. He continues to teach us all along our own journeys into Love.

Enter Joseph. Who is this quiet man, who stands in the background almost unseen? Yet, no small role he played. For, would not Jesus have been considered a bastard, a child who had been conceived in sin, had Joseph not given him his lineage? Here is a man who was in touch with, comfortable with, and with angelic guidance was able to make choices in harmony with the Feminine within him. For men, particularly two thousand years ago, conception, birth, the womb, sexuality, gestation, creative fecundity were all dark, feminine mysteries. Joseph had to go against the natural, masculine response, the expected response of the culture, in order to say his "yes" to Mary, to the will of God.

And, it is Joseph's *yes*—balancing Mary's *yes* to the Holy Spirit—that still astonishes me today. To have quietly divorced Mary, as he had resolved to do out of his unwillingness to put her to shame, would have reflected his just, compassionate, and gentle spirit. Yet, he, being a faith-filled man was receptive to his unconscious, and listened to an angel in a dream—a *numinous* dream so true to his inner being that he could break through the powerful and exclusively masculine traditional, cultural, and religious norms and say, *yes*. What receptivity, gentle strength, faith, integrity, reverence for the Holy, commitment, and courage Joseph exemplified, all traditionally feminine qualities. What a beautiful father and mentor for Jesus: Jesus, who came into life naturally, close to the earth among cows and sheep—close to the bosom of the Mother, the Earth. His birth seems to portend that his mission would include breaking up or, at least, shaking up the patriarchal system: modeling receptivity to the Feminine, inviting everyone to the process of individuation, that we might come into the full potential of who we are called to be.

At least four times Joseph heeded warnings given to him through dreams—a powerful example of a man so in touch with his feminine inner being that, balanced with masculine energy, he could live it fully in the outer world. He was strong enough to move his family to a foreign land; he was wise enough not to return to Israel when through a dream he heard it would be dangerous; and, he was humble enough to settle his family in Nazareth, where they could live in relative quiet and obscurity close to the earth.

Joseph and Mary balanced one another in so many ways. Living out of an integration of the opposites within themselves, what more natural parents could have been chosen to provide a mature and loving home and environment in which Jesus could grow and develop into full maturity? Because they were true to their innermost being, to Divine Love within them, they were indeed a holy family . . . models of family life.

The visit of the Magi to bless this Child seemed also to portend the coming acceptance of the feminine half of consciousness, then, so thoroughly repressed. They are led by a star. Symbolically, the Star can be seen as Light cutting through the darkness (the unconscious), awakening the feminine and portending a giant Awakening of heightened consciousness. Because the Magi, too, listened to the feminine, they heeded the dream warning them not to tell Herod where Jesus was located, thus, saving his life.

And then Herod, who was obviously totally disconnected from the feminine, did what an unbridled masculine is apt to do. He tried to kill off what he saw as a threat to his own power with seemingly no thought or heart for the death, destruction, and dire consequence to others, with no understanding of the terrible injury he inflicted upon his own soul as he wantonly ordered others to kill the children. His inner being must have been severely wounded in that act as well as in the souls of all those who blindly obeyed. This kind of ravaging continues in myriad ways today bringing death and destruction to people all over the world. Jesus' warning comes to mind: "Whatsoever you do to another, you do to yourself."

As I ponder the presentation of Jesus in the temple, I am amazed at how the old scars to the wounded feminine still can get activated and call for immediate forgiveness. "And when the day came for *them* to be purified . . ." and here I note an editorial "them," for according to the Law of Moses, only the mother needed to be purified; the child, however, had to be redeemed. The mother was considered unclean and, presumably, the son was considered tainted by having been within the mother's womb and in contact with her blood, ambiotic and other fluids. Leviticus makes it quite clear:

> If a woman becomes pregnant and gives birth to a *boy*, she will be unclean for *seven* days as when in a state of pollution due to menstruation. On the eighth day the child's foreskin must be

circumcised, and she will wait another *thirty-three* days for her blood to be purified. She will not touch anything consecrated nor go to the sanctuary until the time of her purification is over.

If she gives birth to a *girl*, she will be unclean for *two weeks* as during her monthly periods; and will wait another *sixty-six* days for her blood to be purified. [Both times you will note are doubled for the feminine, who are purified not redeemed.]

When the period of her purification is over, for either boy or girl, she will bring offering, and a young pigeon or turtledove as a *sacrifice for sin.* The priest must offer this before Yahweh, perform the *rite of expiation* for her, and she will be purified from her discharge of blood." [It would seem that woman is considered sinful all the way back to Eve.]

Such is the law concerning a woman who gives birth to either a boy or a girl.

If she cannot afford a lamb, she must take two turtledoves or two young pigeons, one for the burnt offering and the other for the *sacrifice for sin.* The priest will perform the *rite of expiation* and *she will be purified* (Leviticus 12).

Continuing, there is strange and interesting wording in the Law of Moses during the circumcision. "Every male that *opens the womb* shall be called holy or consecrated to the Lord." A psychological understanding may help to clarify this wording: to every male who Awakens to his inner womb, the inner feminine, a fuller, more balanced life will more likely be engendered; he will become more whole, holy, and integrated, and thereby will naturally dedicate himself by honoring the Sacred. For when one lives in harmony through learning to balance the masculine/feminine energies, when one had faced the darkness within and withdrawn their projections from others, then one can but reverence all life and offer himself or herself in Service to the Universe.

Simeon and Anna, who have long awaited this moment, recognize the Child who had been anticipated and was to redeem Jerusalem, which is also a feminine name according to later Scripture. They, too, present feminine qualities: patience . . . awaiting . . . flowing toward the fullness of time . . . allowing the *now* moment to reveal itself. Their intuition, their inner listening, reflect much time spent in solitude, silence, and prayer—all soul qualities of the feminine.

At twelve years of age, Jesus began to assert his masculine qualities. He chose to remain in Jerusalem alone without informing his parents; his focus and aim were clear: he asked questions, sought understanding, and was able to dialogue with those in the temple, presenting his profound thoughts and insights so clearly and with such authority that the elders were amazed. When located by his parents, he answers their concern with an enigmatic question, "Did you not know that I must be in my Father's house?" The process of awakening in consciousness leads to an understanding and integration of the past. Jesus learned the history of the people, religion, traditions, and culture. He became steeped in the patriarchy and Scripture. As he increased in wisdom and stature over the ensuing years, surely, a great sorting and discernment process was gestating within him.

In the New Testament, Mark's short gospel was written first and begins with a mature John preaching in the wilderness. John, who lived humbly, close to nature and the earth appears to be well integrated, notwithstanding his appearance and eating habits, that were likely to have been seen as bizarre, even irrational. Yet, he was able to express who he was with great authority in the world. He knew his mission and he fulfilled it to the end. As a messenger he preached with such vigor, assertion, clarity and charisma, the people flocked to hear him.

As he baptized with water, he spoke of the One who would come and baptize with Fire . . . the refining Fire that is crucial to the transformative process, the Fire that burns away the chaff and dross of the false self and leaves the gold of the individual essence. Surrender, letting go, forgiveness, patience, and trust aid immeasurably in allowing the searing Fire of Divine Love to do its inner Work.

John had no problem in being assertive and clear with the Pharisees and Sadducees, who were definitely steeped in the patriarchal establishment. He constantly returned to an emphasis on "bearing good fruit." This, according to John, comes about by sharing one's goods and being just in one's work—once again the balance.

Then came the moment that John and the people had been awaiting. Jesus came to the Jordan to be baptized by water. He, too, chose to be baptized in the water, symbolic of the feminine unconscious, whereupon the Spirit of God descended like a dove and alighted upon him. Is this not a great moment of revelation? Is the Godhead giving approval for what is to come: the breakthrough integration of the Feminine into the world?

And while Jesus is being led in Matthew's and Luke's gospels, or driven in Mark's gospel into the wilderness to be tempted by the devil, John is arrested and locked in prison. The authorities arrest him and "shut him up": the feminine energies of wilderness, water, and what seems like "irrational" behavior seemed to be too much. Symbols carry a power that is difficult, if not impossible, to measure; they work in the depths of people's psyches. And, once again, Herod's fear of losing his authoritative power thrust him into making another violent decision that ultimately cost John his life.

Meanwhile, Jesus is in the wilderness to be tempted by the devil. Now "devil" is an interesting word in that spelled backward it is "lived," just as "evil"—the devil's work, we are taught—is "live" spelled backward. Yet, in fact, to follow the devil's enticements is to turn away from authentic living. This may give a clue to the real confrontation Jesus, and each of us at some point in our lives, is to have with the devil: a discernment process in which one makes the choice to live backward toward yesterday's will of God, toward a living death; or, chooses a life-giving, uncharted direction that may lead to unknown vistas.

Jesus later would spend forty days and forty nights discerning his mission: a balanced process that involves his rational faculties as well as his intuitive qualities. He struggled with the devil in this wild feminine setting. He also confronted the beasts that roam the land as well as his own inner "wild beasts" along with those in the collective unconscious. The choices he made during that time illustrate the values we, too, are to embody if we are to live authentically by following our own deep intuition and the spiritual guidance that comes from listening to the Voice of Wisdom in times of solitude, silence, prayer, and surrender.

After the angels came and ministered to him, Jesus set out to begin the ministry for which he was sent. After preaching in Galilee, he returned to Nazareth, and teaching in the synagogue, he announced through reading from the book of Isaiah exactly what the focus of his life would be: to preach good news to the poor, the disenfranchised, which included women, and also, by implication, the feminine principle within all men. He was to proclaim release to the captives, those in prison and to all who are bound by their ego-fears. He healed the blind, which can also be taken in a symbolic way: the blindness of the patriarchy to the harmonizing energies of the feminine. Jesus also saw the need to set at liberty those who are oppressed: the minorities, women, the Feminine . . . and to proclaim the acceptable year of the Lord— *now*, or whenever, wherever, these prophecies and promises are being lived out.

As long as Jesus kept within the prescribed masculine boundaries, the people marveled at the wisdom and gracious words that proceeded out of his mouth. When they questioned his authority, he reminded them of the prophets Elijah and Elisha:

In the days of Elijah, a famine had come over the earth. She was parched because "the heavens were shut up"; the masculine heavens had withheld the nourishment of rain so necessary for the earth to flourish. Elijah had said, "By the life of Yahweh . . . there will be neither dew nor rain these coming years unless I give the word" (I Kings 17:1). Even the streams dried up. This is what happens when the Feminine is ignored: the flow and fructification of life dries up.

Elijah was sent by God not to those the people would have expected; rather, he sought out a woman, a widow, in the land of Sidonia. The woman shared her food and water with Elijah, notwithstanding they were the last morsels she had. Elijah, in turn, provided her with a jar of meal and a jug of oil that were replenished as used, exemplifying another feminine principle: *the more you let go of, the more is returned to you.* Later, when the widow's son fell ill and died, Elijah confronted the masculine

Yahweh in prayer and, through Elijah's feminine ministration, the child's soul came back into his body and he was healed (I Kings 17:7–24).

Then, Jesus reminded the people gathered in the synagogue of how Naaman, who had leprosy, was healed by Elisha. A little girl was the messenger that sent Naaman through his master, the King of Aram, to seek healing from the King of Israel. The king, who was clearly out of touch with his feminine energies, immediately experienced this as a tremendous threat. But Elisha, a prophet well in touch with his Inner Being, calmly takes charge. He tells Naaman to bathe seven times in the Jordan. Naaman, who is the army commander, became enraged. This seemed too easy, not manly enough. Yet, when chided by a servant, he went and immersed himself in the waters, the healing feminine waters, and he was cleansed, now having flesh "like that of a little child."

When Elisha would accept no payment, Naaman presented Elisha's servant with as much earth as two mules could carry. Naaman, having been healed by the Feminine was now able to offer Her, albeit symbolically, as gift (11 Kings 5:1–19).

Jesus' recalling of these two prophets suggests to the people, both consciously and unconsciously, that he is claiming to have the same Power, Source, and Authority. He, too, will be a prophet bringing healing, life, light, and the Feminine energies into the darkness of an imbalanced world. Seething with rage, denying his gifts, and filled with fear, the masculine authorities attempt to take Jesus out of the city to throw him over a cliff. So blind are they with wrath, Jesus passes through the midst of them and leaves (Matthew 13:54–58; Mark 6:1–6; Luke 4:16–30).

Afterwards, when walking by the sea of Galilee, Jesus calls the first disciples. The first two are brothers, Peter and Andrew, and then two other brothers, James and John. All of these men are fishermen, who provide food for the nourishment of others. Living close to the sea, these are strong, virile men, who reached down in the depths of the water, mended nets, and cleaned the fish. These men were balanced and intimately in touch with the feminine through their daily work. Quick to follow their intuition, they each cut through any rational, masculine obstacles;

spontaneously, and with trust, they leave with Jesus without turning back (Matthew 4:18–22, Mark 1:16–20).

When they went to Capernaum on the Sabbath, Jesus entered the synagogue and taught. Once again, the people were astonished at his teaching and authority, not as the Scribes taught. True authority is recognized wherever the masculine and feminine are authentically in balance within an individual, when the ego-fears and the hidden gifts of the unconscious have been acknowledged and integrated. Jesus was and *is* the model of the individuated consciousness; the scribes were victims of the imbalanced energies and unfaced depths; their outer persona was who they thought they were. The people seemed to recognize the difference (Mark 1:21–22; Luke 4:31–32; Matthew 7:28–29).

In the synagogue, a man with an unclean spirit cries out, "What have you to do with us, Jesus of Nazareth?" Being in an assembly of people, could this man be representing a collective masculine shadow fearful of the Light that will awaken the feminine consciousness? Was Jesus' higher consciousness too much for him to bear? Jesus rebukes the unclean spirit, telling it to be silent and to come forth out of the man. And, instantly, with a loud cry, the man was healed. Jesus' very presence seemed to evoke the predominantly masculine fears toward the feminine. As these fears arise, Jesus meets them face-to-face and dispels them. Facing the demons is an important step in the long, continuous road toward the goal of wholeness for individuals and a people, i.e., humanity: another step for Jesus on the road to Jerusalem and the Cross, where the ultimate transformation takes place.

After casting out the demon in the synagogue, Jesus goes to Simon and Andrew's house with James and John. There, they found Simon's mother-in-law in bed and ill with a high fever . . . she was "burning up, angry" according to one definition of "fever." Jesus touched her hand and lifted her up, and the fever left. In this simple, nourishing act, Jesus demonstrates to his first four disciples the feminine touch that balances the masculine action of raising others up, be it from illness, anger, abuse, oppression, or life itself. And then, she, in turn, having been ministered to, is able to serve them. With and in Jesus, we see over and over again the harmony and inner peace that follows when one is able to hold the tension of the opposites in balance.

When the demons recognized Jesus by the Light that penetrated through the walls of fear, their power dissipated; they had to obey his command to leave, his injunction not to speak or to make him known. For when light enters a room of darkness, the darkness can no longer exist there. Because of the extreme repression of the Feminine, I wonder if the psyches of the people must have been collectively a breeding ground for the demons. Right from the beginning of his Work, Jesus began to release those in the bondage of darkness and fear (Matthew 8:24–27; Mark 1:29–34; Luke 4:38–41).

The next morning, Jesus arose and went to a lonely place to pray. He knew well the balance of doing and being. He knew that times of silence and solitude were essential to remain in harmony with the Power that flowed through him; and, he willingly opened himself to the Wisdom within. Out of these times of attunement, letting-go, and emptying-out, he was nourished and filled with whatever he would need, wherever he might be. Even then, finding times and places to be alone and silent was difficult. The crowds sought him out, so great were their needs. Yet, Jesus would stay in one place for only a day or so before leaving, continuing "on the road" to share with and awaken others to the good news . . . the purpose for which he had come. He and the disciples traveled to town after town throughout all of Galilee (Mark 1:35–38; Luke 4:42–43).

Jesus spent a great deal of time near the water. When the people pressed upon him by the Gennesaret Lake, he got into Simon's empty boat; while the men were washing nets, he taught the people from the boat. When he finished speaking, he told Simon to "put out into the deep and let out the nets for a catch." Simon reminded Jesus that they had toiled all night and had caught nothing. Jesus' way was that of intuition, while they had been toiling to no avail. And by listening and following Jesus with blind trust: "At your word, I will do it," the catch was amazing! They filled the two empty boats until they were close to sinking. This feminine way seemed almost too much for Simon Peter and he told Jesus to depart—a scene that will be repeated with the opposite happening toward the end of Jesus' physical life when he tells Peter, "Begone!"

Here, Jesus reassures Peter with a theme that continues throughout his lifetime, "Do not be afraid," and then, so quietly as to be almost unnoticed, he announces the mission of the disciples: "Henceforth you will be fishers of people." In Jungian terminology, they will cast their nets deep into the psyches of others, to raise up that which has been veiled and hidden, notably, the Feminine, with the promise of much fish, good nourishment, for themselves and others (Luke 5:1–11; Mark 1:16–20; Matthew 4:18–32).

Before Jesus' teaching of what we now call the Beatitudes, *Be-attitudes*, he went to the mountains or hills to pray. He went to a masculine high place to go into the feminine deep well within to pray. Each one of the be-attitudes is also a study in the balance of the opposites:

- *to become poor is to become rich;*
- *to mourn leads to being comforted;*
- *to be meek is to be given the earth;*
- *to be hungry and thirsty leads to satisfaction and to being nourished;*
- *to be merciful is to obtain mercy; we receive that which we give;*
- *to be pure in heart is to know the abiding Indwelling Presence;*
- *to be a peacemaker is to become a co-creator in the Divine Plan;*
- *to weep now is to laugh later;*
- *to be persecuted for good is to be blessed inwardly.*

To be all of the above in daily life is what will lead one to gladness and joy in that inward Center or Stillpoint within which each individual can come to live, the true Reality of the heart in an ego-driven world . . . a blessed oasis and, ultimately, our Home and heaven, as we journey into Love (Matthew 5:1–12; Luke 6:12, 20–23).

Jesus is very clear that he did not come to abolish the law and prophets, but to fulfill them . . . to bring them to fullness. Although the more masculine "Thou shall not" injunctions or commandments of the canon of Hebrew Scripture may remain true, the more feminine be-attitudes acknowledge be-ing and blessing as equally true. Jesus' life will bear witness to this balance to the very end. The parables on salt and light come together in Matthew's gospel as another example of this harmony: enjoining those who would hear to be "salt of the earth" and "light to the world."

When Jesus speaks of murder and even of angry fear-thoughts against another, his way of reconciliation is feminine. He advises against going to the judge or magistrate, the accepted masculine authority for settling disputes in those times. Rather, he suggests that two individuals are capable of sharing their differences and finding a mutual solution. He also implies that as long as we are not in harmony with our brothers and sisters, our gifts cannot be freely and fully offered in service to the Blessed One.

On adultery, Jesus makes it clear that to look or to think of another with inappropriate desire is as if to commit the act, that thoughts matter and have consequences that extend out to others. He emphasizes the point by suggesting that those offending parts be excised. To dehumanize the Feminine seems to be equal to masculine mutilation (Matthew 5:27–30; 18:8–9; Mark 9:43–48).

Jesus' clarity of thought-forms seems never to have been given due consideration. According to Jesus and through lived experience, thoughts *are equal* to action; they render us vulnerable. When we begin to recognize that our thoughts *are* just as much our prayer as the times we take specifically "to pray," isn't it tremendously relevant to notice our thoughts and just what it is we are drawing to ourselves, not to mention what we are sending out into the world? We do well to ask our selves from time to time, "How much time am I spending in fear thoughts . . . angry thoughts . . . jealous and envy thoughts . . . greed thoughts . . . vengeful thoughts . . . lustful thoughts . . . negative thinking, compared to prayerful, grateful, praise thoughts?

Do we carefully consider the thought forms that we take into ourselves as we watch television, movies, the ads, or as we read books, magazines, newspapers? The daily news in so much of the media is filled with violence and dehumanizing stories – fear thoughts sent out for the world to absorb like sponges. And when we subject our selves to this bombardment of darkness, can we move from the ways of masculine thinking, analyzing, critical modalities to the feminine heart held, compassionate way-of-being?

When I forget to "pray the news" and allow myself to get caught up in all the violence being expressed, my dreams, my thoughts, and my imagination become fear-filled and my blood pressure goes up. Then I am but another channel for extending disharmony out to the world and miss the opportunity to extend forgiveness, hope, and love. We are just as much at danger when we absorb violent fear thoughts as we are when we inhale the poison of another's cigarette smoke. What we are not awakened to can do great damage to our psyches in the same way that violence in the streets can kill our bodies. The massive preponderance of violent, unbridled sexual, and other destructive energies being emitted at every moment is an aberrant consequence of the great imbalance of the masculine and feminine energies that, when integrated, can give birth to peace, justice, and harmony in the world.

And can we truly abandon ourselves into the Heart of Love in prayer if we spend the greater part of our lives almost oblivious to the ongoing stream of semi-conscious inner dialogue? To pray continuously is to be totally awake to, and mindful of, the present reality, moment by moment. We need, perhaps, at least as much as food fasting, to take ample time for mind fasting, time to be still, empty of thought, so we might recognize the living and loving Companion Presence that dwells within our hearts and will gently guide us as we ask.

Returning to Scripture, when Jesus speaks of divorce, he is an advocate for women in those patriarchal times. A man had the right to dismiss or to divorce *his* woman or wife for the love of another woman, for something as commonplace as her cooking. At best, a woman had few rights and no recourse; her plight was harsher than ever should she be divorced. Jesus recognized women as individuals with inalienable rights, rather than as chattel or objects for bringing sons into the world and simply to meet a man's sexual desires. Jesus treated men and women equally (Matthew 5:31–32; 19:9; Mark 10:11–12; Luke 16–18).

Jesus' injunction not to swear an oath using the Divine Name, but simply to say yes or no, once again reveals his simplicity and humility; the recognition that one can only make their vow, state their truth, out of an inner integrity that comes from the heart. He specifically states, "Do not swear by your head" (Matthew 5:33–37).

While meditating on this passage, a scene from one of the most difficult moments of my life came to mind. I was to be the key witness at a very painful criminal trial in which I loved both parties, a trial in which the parameters were not all that clear. The thought of placing my hand on the Bible and swearing that I would "tell the truth, the whole truth and nothing but the truth, so help me God" undid me. Who was I, whose testimony was to have a significant effect on the outcome, to presume that I knew the whole truth? I recognized that I could not with any integrity take such an oath and I refused. To my surprise and gratitude the judge allowed me to state what I had suggested: I would simply tell the "truth" of the situation as I had witnessed and experienced it. This helped me understand the wisdom of Jesus' injunction.

How common it is to hear flippant oaths such as "I swear to God," "so help me God," or "swearing on a stack of Bibles" spoken mindlessly, as if to use God or Scripture will give credence and power to one's own view or behavior. Yet, the swearing of a vow whether on the Bible, Qu'ran, or some sacred object with sincerity and reverence does make an emphatic statement and promise, and could well be an appropriate ritual when called for.

How difficult it is to have the inner integrity of heart that Jesus lived when the feminine has been and continues to be so violated and repressed in the world. The exploitation of the feminine qualities inevitably leads to the diminishment of the masculine. Imbalanced masculine energy seems to equate itself with

God, thereby competing with God and attempting to use God for its own purposes, i.e., rather than stewarding the earth with great care and consideration, the ongoing ravaging and raping of her body is a terrible affront to the feminine and to the whole ecology of the earth—to our peril. On the other hand, when the feminine and masculine energies are in harmony, cooperation and co-creation with the Divine Architect can become possible with mutual blessing to all.

Jesus takes the patriarchal Hebrew Scripture's injunction, "an eye for an eye and a tooth for a tooth," of Exodus, Leviticus, and Deuteronomy, and completely reverses it. He moves from the rational-masculine modality to the feminine-heart response: to turn the other cheek when struck, to give more than asked for when sued, to walk two miles if you are forced to go one, to give to those who beg or steal or ask to borrow. This way-of-being did not make sense to people two thousand years ago. We continue to miss the point today. When an unbalanced act of masculine aggressiveness occurs, a feminine response allows the situation to return to balance. The opposites are no longer opposed. It must be said that similar disruptive consequences occur with unbridled, unbalanced feminine energies.

Jesus follows this teaching about retaliation with even more difficult enjoiners: to love one's enemies; to do good to those who hate you; to bless those who curse you; to pray for those who abuse you. It is easy to love those who love you in return, those with whom you have much in common socially, economically, religiously, politically, vocationally. Yet, as affirming and nurturing as this may be, the potential for growth is limited within the narrow confines of mutuality. Jesus knew well that the development of mercy, compassion, inner peace, joy, justice, and wholeness arises in facing what is hidden in the darkness. Thus, this compost of ego-fear, doubt, and guilt extends out to others from the unconscious depth of each individual. This includes the unlovable, unredeemed parts of our psyche and, perhaps more importantly, the gold of our unrealized gifts, our creative, fertile potentials awaiting birth (Mt. 5:43–48; Luke 6:27–28, 32–36).

What might happen if, when we see and hear of the ravages of war on TV, or read of one more violent crime, or agonize over the abused and the oppressed in so many nations, we were to re-image the situation in the light of Jesus' injunction to love our enemies? Aren't we profoundly touched when we learn of someone who lives this out in the world, as Mother Teresa so powerfully modeled as she embraced those the world would turn from?

Most of us freely and enthusiastically respond naturally to others' needs that come into our awareness; some make it a way of life. The danger is that we can so easily become paralyzed, apathetic, or overwhelmed by the sheer numbers of possible issues and needs that confront us today. However, as simplistic as it may sound, we need over and over again to recall that we are one light of billions of lights in the darkness of life's illusions and challenges; we *can* stay shining as we meet the challenges that life sets at our particular door or in our heart.

Who can deny that wars arise from and are fought with unrestrained masculine energy, whether men or women are the warriors? The weaponry is grossly phallic from swords, knives, and the smallest pistols to the stealth bombers and rocket projectories—power and sexuality gone awry . . . masculine energy asserting itself under many guises with the aim to kill, to garner, to feel man's power in a communal and "socially acceptable" way.

It is not surprising that during conflicts and war many individuals anguishing over the slaughter are taking a stance that calls upon feminine energy for balance, whether they realize the implication or not. One friend, Patricia Dorsey, was compelled during Desert Storm to go to her room, to close the door, and to pray and weep for the entire weeks of the onslaught. In her despair over the innocent lives of our "enemies" being negligently wasted, she developed a need to express the horror that welled up through those long days and nights. She drew upon Scripture as she began to draw fragments of broken lives and turn them into postcards to send out to the world. Her *WordArt*, as it came to be known, was not easy to look at. For, she hid not the graphic fear and pain the people were experiencing. The proceeds from her creative response to the *de-creation* that war brings were given to appropriate sources as one individual's expression of grief.

We live with growing peril until we begin to face our nations growing arrogance and greed and stop projecting our own darkness on to an enemy. This is in no way to condone the evil another nation may be perpetrating; it is to admit and confess that the enemy is also us. We will not be able to own up to our national shadow (never mind befriend our own inner and outer enemies!) until we reconstitute and re-embrace the feminine energy so long held in the bondage of ego-fear and ignorance! Still, the voices and votes of the people are now casting doubts and disapproval as to the efficacy and morality of war. We may be waking up at last!

On giving alms and on praying, Jesus once again favors the feminine way. Rather than speaking out and showing others our goodness and piety, we are invited to be silent, to offer our gifts and our prayers in the secret closet of our heart (Matthew 6:1–8).

What we have come to call "The Lord's Prayer" is basically a prayer on the need for forgiveness. In fact, forgiveness is the only part of the prayer in Mark's gospel; it appears later as an explanation for the withered fig tree. In Luke's gospel, the prayer is placed between his discourse with Mary and Martha and the parable of the friend at midnight. Again, the focus is on forgiveness.

Matthew's version of the prayer is the one prayed by Christians throughout the world day and night. The prayer is addressed in this patriarchal setting to the Father in the masculine heaven. "Hallowed be your Name." Up until this time, God's name, Yahweh, was not to be spoken. Jesus not only calls upon God's name, he calls God "Father," which in the Aramaic language conveys the message of Abba, "daddy," a familial parental appellation. Still, Jesus is ever reverent as he implies: let us come to know You, that we might bless, worship, and praise You for all of Creation, which includes and embraces everything, everyone.

Next, and paraphrased here, Jesus prays that Abba's realm come, Abba's Will be done, on earth *as it is* in the heavenly realms . . . again the balance. Then, when Jesus asks for daily bread, he might well have remembered the devil's invitation to turn stones into bread. Jesus affirms that bread is everyone's daily need, which can be understood by at least three possible meanings: that of sufficient nourishment for the body, that of spiritual nourishment, and that of our work in the world. As Jesus in the wilderness demonstrates, we are to be nourished by a process of kneading the ingredients of our lives, taking times of waiting in the silence, and of being refined by fire *so that* we can be blessed, our hearts broken open, and our lives shared with others as blessing, healing, and nourishment.

The rest of the prayer teaches us about the efficacy of forgiveness. Our lives are stunted when we hold onto our hurts and wounds, bypassing the healing balm of forgiveness. We are forgiven to the degree we are able to forgive ourselves and others. For, if our hearts are clogged with resentment and bitterness, which will surely turn in upon ourselves, how can we receive the blessing of forgiveness that Abba is always bestowing upon us? Harmony, peace, and balance come only when the giving and receiving of forgiveness is mutual. In my experience, forgiveness of our mistakes through the Spirit is a most effective way for ego-illusions and fear to be dispelled, for peace to be regained.

Just imagine how the words of Jesus' prayer must have shocked the people—especially the Pharisees, scribes, lawyers, Sadduces, and priests. What an affront to their piety to hear the God of Abraham addressed as Abba. Do we really *hear* and accept the amazing revelation that we are intimately related to, One with, the Divine Father and, I will add, the Divine Mother; or, the Divine Mind and the Divine Heart of Love.

As I reflect on the energies of the masculine and feminine, terms like "the battle of the sexes," "the war between heaven and earth" arise. Isn't it time for the battles to cease, so that peace can come upon the land? I had the image of a sculpted bust, which usually includes the human head, neck, shoulders, and chest cut off at the heart. While this masculine "bust" has been embraced in Western culture for centuries, the feminine has been denigrated to the sexual symbols of breast, genitals, and legs. When we symbolically cut the body in two pieces and reverence all the masculine head qualities and objectify the feminine heart qualities, the results are disastrous. We cannot but be aware of how far this has brought us toward rampant sexual abuse, injustice, oppression—and worse, toward global genocide and geocide, the destroying of the earth and its myriad creatures. If forgiveness is Jesus' unequivocal answer to this dilemma, we must begin with ourselves. If our hearts are filled with fears, doubts, and ego-illusions, we are but dim lights and conditional love in and to the world.

I once naively wrote a letter to First Lady Pat Nixon just prior to the Watergate scandal, and gave a format for a national healing service to be offered on television for the forgiveness of our nation for all its transgressions: for our arrogance, racism, and greed, for our turning our backs to the poor, for the early genocide of Native Americans, for slavery, for our exploitation of other nations when it serves "our interests;" the list could be embarrassingly and appallingly long. She never answered and I certainly understand. But I still think spiritually, this could give us a fresh start. We are long overdue for a national cleansing and reawakening of the intrinsic values upon which this country was founded.

Since we are the richest nation in the world with unlimited potential, we have yet to tap more fully into our human gifts, and to accept that we have a great responsibility to exemplify to the world our original values of sharing, equal rights, and justice for *all*. This is not to belittle the many efforts we do make on behalf of others, our humanitarian efforts in many international crises, the blessed, generous, and gracious gifts of philanthropists, and the generous giving of ordinary citizens. Still, the transgressions of our nation are many from its discovery to the present time of war, disasters, and immorality: the masculine-feminine energies remain out of balance even though the two are inexorably linked!

"Do not be anxious." After all this time, Jesus' injunction has hardly been heard. For, how many among us live stress-free lives abandoning ourselves into the hands of the Blessed One, trusting the Process, and flowing in harmony with the universe? Do we not toil and compete in order to reap and store more and more things? Our lives are, more often than not, geared to masculine values from birth to death. And, how much of big business would be out of business if the people of the nation were not so anxious and fearful of not having enough; enough variety, enough of whatever is advertised, enough of what others have, enough money, enough diversion?

Jesus knew well that anxiety and fear were the greatest obstacles to realizing the fullness of life. That we are One with the Power that created us was a given for Jesus. That all our needs are available before we even ask when we are not in fear, he did not question. Jesus was so free of fear that he expected to be Divinely guided and protected; he made choices that were in keeping with his mission. He was open to the Power and Wisdom that flowed through him at every moment; and, he lived by a feminine process of *be*-ing, out of which his appropriate masculine *do*-ing manifested. This way-of-being in the world gets blocked and paralyzed by fear, anxiety and doubt. "Do not be anxious." Be free to *be!* (Matthew 6:25–34; Luke 12:22–31).

When Jesus discourses on judging others, he recognizes that propensity of human nature to project onto others what we are blind to in the depths of our own unconscious. Hence, he exhorts us to look carefully within—not just on the surface of life, but to the feminine secret places of the heart, where our spiritual eyes are reflectors of our soul, before judging or condemning another with attacking masculine energy. This is not only kind and appropriate, but also in our own best interest. For when we judge others, we are most often saying far more about ourselves than those whom we condemn. Truly, the log in our own eye will invariably keep us from seeing clearly. We hate or fear in others what we are blind to in ourselves and would rather not admit or see, and it seems to be no easy task to remove logs from eyes. Jesus sums up this efficacy of balance in what we have come to know as the Golden Rule (Matthew 7:1–5, 12; Luke 6:31, 37–38, 41–42).

"Enter by the narrow gate." And what is this narrow gate that leads to life? Jesus modeled this throughout his life, and it is crucial that we, like Jesus, be led or driven to our days and nights in the wilderness. For, the narrow gate implies that we cannot get through it carrying much baggage. It implies simplicity, calling for a willingness to take the necessary time in silence and solitude, to delve deeply into the storehouse of our own inner baggage, to sort out the piles of ego-fear, doubt, and guilt from the past and collective expectations which are stored away in the darkness and holding us in bondage. It also implies commitment to the process; "the way *is* hard" until we are free, unburdened, and able to live as co-creators on earth. No surprise that "those who find it are few!"

Yet, we are always being invited and shown the way through the narrow gate, the gate to simplicity, silence, times of solitude, as we become awakened in Consciousness. When our outer life reflects an inner integrity freed from the prison of fear and ignorance, we have entered that gate; we live in harmony and balance knowing our Oneness with all of creation. We become beneficial presences in the world wherever we may be (Matthew 7:13–14; Luke 13:23–24).

As you read *Journey into Love*, it will help to be mindful of this introduction, which offers an overview of one of the most extraordinary gifts that Jesus bestowed on humanity through his words and deeds: the balancing of the dominant, masculine energies with the feminine energies so long repressed. This theme overshadows the whole Story, sometimes subtly, sometimes overtly. I pray each reader will find some new insights, plenty of things to ponder, some spiritual nourishment, and perhaps, even some inspiration. May we be united on the Journey through our fears into the Heart of Love. In the Silence,

Nan

1

The Road to Damascus

Love is born anew in each one of us as we enter life here on earth, born with an implicit hope that we shall come to live into and share the LoveConsciousness dormant within our heart and soul, that we might fulfill the potential our birth portends. Yet, for much of the first half of our lives, many of us learn to build walls, to construct inner-defense systems, to prefer worldly delights, so much so, we risk losing ourselves to the world's spell. We are robots unaware. Fear lurks in most of us as an energy-zapping, yet more often than not, unacknowledged, companion.

As good people, we learn to do the right things all too often for the wrong reasons. Like Saul of Tarsus, we take too much competitive pride in our achievements, our families, our work, our religious tradition, our country. We become the people Jesus met with compassion and ministered to: the blind and deaf, the sick, the paralyzed, the dead. We become the disciples, the woman at the well, the Pharisees, priests, lawyers, and scribes. Each parable is meant to be in a real sense our story; each parable can become our growing edge, a catalyst for transformation.

Even in the most loving families, life can conspire to deaden the Spirit at work within us. Siblings, school experiences, illness, friendships, deaths, prejudice, oppression, injustice—all have the potential to wound our psyches. We all fall from the garden of innocence—some more, some less. Like many of us, I made an unconscious defense pact early in life to relieve the fears that had begun to grow within me. As all too often happens, I became good, quiet, whatever "they" wanted me to be—outwardly. And inwardly, I lived in a world of my own making, one which included those I loved and annihilated those I feared. I could be and do anything I wanted in this secret inner world; I felt powerful. Sadly, however, the carefree, spontaneous child began to withdraw, stifled with fear. As I built an inner wall solid as brick, the wondrous creative flow of my birthright became blocked.

Grace is pure mystery, pure gift. I shall forever be grateful for the blessing of Awakening that She bestowed on me almost forty years ago. My husband, Ray, and I were living in Florida with our five beautiful children, the sixth Navy move in twelve years. Outwardly, I seemed happy. I could not imagine there was anymore to life. Yet, inwardly, my spirit was restless; something was missing. Then, quite unexpectedly and unbidden, I began waking up somewhere between two and four each morning. I would arise, go into one of the children's bedrooms and stare out of the window.

One special star, the Day Star, I believe, became so familiar and personal, I began to think of it as "my" star; I would simply *be* with that star for close to an hour and then return to bed. Strangely, I never questioned this ritual that for many months became as routine as brushing my teeth: meditating (though I had never heard of that word in the 1960s) in silence and solitude, praying without words, sending out, albeit unconsciously, a great Cry from the depths of my being.

Then, without warning, I *awakened* one morning to find myself living in a radically new way-of-being in the world. Gone was the robotic existence, gone was my need to be understood, gone were my inner fears and restlessness. The only word that comes close to describing the deep peace and quiet joy that enveloped me like a cocoon, and which I could feel radiating out from me, is Love. Everything within me and all I experienced without flowed. I felt totally in harmony with the universe. Yet, so long had I lived accepting all that the winds blew through my life, that I lived in this state of "grace" for ten days, assuming that I was somehow responsible for it. It felt so natural, as if I'd known it as a child or in some other distant place.

Though I dreaded going out-of-doors in Florida, even the heavy, hot humid air of summer now seemed in balance with nature's harmony. The grass, flowers, and trees seemed transparent—shimmering with colors that radiated and defined each blade, petal, and leaf. I could *see* how each aspect fit into the Whole and I felt grateful to be a participant in Life's abundant, glorious, and wondrous beauty. I could *feel* how I participate in the Oneness, the interconnectedness, of *all* people, *all* things.

Never in those ten days did I hear an unkind word nor did I feel antipathy toward anyone or anything—in fact, quite the opposite. My husband, the children, friends, strangers, and I all seemed to be in harmony with one another and with all of Creation. While shopping, I was not surprised to have strangers stop to share their stories and concerns with me; nor was I surprised that I responded naturally with deep understanding and compassion. My shyness was gone. Like the single leaf on a tree dancing in the breeze, I saw each person I encountered as a totally unique individual, yet part of a beautiful whole. There was a Unity of Being that brought tears to my eyes and a terrible yearning.

During those days, I remember driving home with the family from a day at the beach and wondering at the camaraderie between us. Often, from 4:30 until dinnertime life was chaotic and unpleasant—especially after an all-day outing. Yet here we were confined in a hot, sandy car in city traffic sharing happy memories of other places we had lived. When we stopped for a red light on a wooden bridge, my eyes locked with the sad eyes of an old man standing by the rail. All at once I seemed to sense this man's pain or loneliness, and I sent him energy waves of love; I felt he received my offering and knew me as well. It was a Unity with another that I had not known before of soul-meeting-soul in silence. Though the honking of horns in cars behind us suddenly broke the Meeting, I can still close my eyes and recapture those timeless moments.

Then one morning, I sensed something amiss as I awakened. Gone was the envelope of Love; gone was the inner peace and harmony. It was as if the lens of my inner eye, which had been clearly in focus, had suddenly become distorted and clouded. For days I grieved, not knowing or understanding the loss. What I did realize was that there was no way that I would be willing to tolerate the old way of being, the robot like life. I had tasted heaven on earth; I *knew* as I had always sensed that there was far more to life. I had been shown a dazzling and profound dimension to living, and I was determined to discover how to return to what seemed to be heaven on earth.

I can point to this period as a rebirth, as a reawakening of the Child within me, as an invitation to a more conscious journey: *the* Journey! I now understand that until we become as children, we miss the freedom, harmony, peace, and joy awaiting us in the realm of True Life. Then, I only knew that somehow life was far more magnificent than I had known for much of my life. I had forgotten my childhood sense of joy, delight, play, spontaneity, and friendship with nature as walls of fear, distractions, defenses, and *busyness* grew. I was faced with hard questions. Where do I go with this life-changing gift? Who could help me claim it, renew it? Years of not being heard or understood, even of being thought crazy, compelled me to be silent, to withdraw inwardly and to begin a process of denial. I told no one, not even Ray, of these wonder-filled days.

Yet, as Mechtild of Magdeburg said, "The day of my spiritual awakening was the day I saw—and knew I saw—all things in God and God in all things." Everything else suddenly fell into perspective in the light of this awareness. In time, I was to discover that once Life had found me, once Love had taken me by the hand, there was no way I could stop the inner pilgrimage. Though the journey would entail incredible times of struggle, pain, and sacrifice, I was, without doubt, on the Way. There was no turning back.

Saul, who became known as Paul, was blinded on the road to Damascus so that he could begin to see. For each of us, the experience on this road is different. For many, it is a gradual process into new life, a journey something like that of Nicodemus, of struggling to understand what Jesus meant by saying:

> *In all truth I tell you,*
>> *No one can enter the Kindom[3] of God without*
>> *Being born from above, without*
>> *Being born through water and the Spirit;*
>> *What is born of human nature is human;*
>> *What is born of the Spirit is spirit.*
>>
>> John 3:3–6

For others, conversion comes through trauma and suffering. However it comes, Awakening is an ongoing journey. To begin to see and to turn our lives around is only the beginning. As an act of the soul, conversion calls us to take a long, loving, and sometimes painful look at who we are and whom we have been. This road humbles us and gives us strength to repent, to ask forgiveness, to simplify and discard all that is not Life-giving, and to abandon ourselves into Love's hands. And, inasmuch as we are able to affirm our *yes* and, as we are guided to walk the roads that Jesus walked in harmony with today's world, we are blessed with new life, new peace, new joy, new love . . . and freedom.

Only slowly have I learned to make this journey with a bit of grace. For years I fought the process, stumbled and fell, rebelled and strayed, regressed, and betrayed my inner being—and yet, always the gifts of forgiveness, strength, courage, guidance, and Unconditional Love have been given whenever I have had the humility to ask, to listen for the Voice of Wisdom, and to respond.

I've been given answers to many unvoiced questions on this pilgrimage. I've learned to love and to trust the Mystery not needing to know the future. I no longer take Grace for granted—it is pure gift. I've accepted that my essential course of action is simply *to be* in the Eternal Now, ready to follow the small, still Voice heard in the Silence. With the help of more individuals than I could count, who have inspired and guided me, I've walked through my fears.[4] To be freed from fear has brought liberation and the joy of loving and living with profound simplicity, with a sense of kinship with nature.

A difficult mixed blessing is to *see* the terrible—sometimes horrific and unconscionable—injustice that plagues our world and planet. To be in this world, but not of it, one becomes freer to serve toward its healing and renewal. This growing and maturing of our soul and spirit is a door that is open to all people everywhere. To choose Life with deep conviction and commitment is one of the greatest gifts we can give ourselves, our families, our global neighbors, as well as the planet and all creatures. As we move toward recognizing and extending our innate wholeness and holiness, the ripple effect is more powerful than we could ever ask for or imagine.

Now, when I talk about being in harmony with the universe and my friends chuckle and roll their eyes at me, I smile. For, since discovering Who I am and Whose I am, I no longer need others to understand me. Wonder has become a friend—from the simplicity of each day's unfolding to the marvelous complexity of how interdependent we are with one another and all of Creation. Gratitude is now a constant companion as I continue to grow along the pathways that Jesus extends to all. I know through experience that we are never alone. For deep within the Sacred Chapel of our heart, Love's Companioning Presence dwells in and among each one of us!

2

Preparation for the Journey

$\mathcal{I}$n the beginning was LoveConsciousness, and LoveConsciousness was with God, and LoveConsciousness was God." Such is John 1:1 paraphrased. LoveConsciousness is ever with us. Each one of us is a blessed heir of the Creator called to be a unique expression of Love and Light, an individual consciousness within the body of Christ Consciousness. A delightfully refreshing answer to the question, "Who are you?" was given by Edmund West, Canon at the Cathedral of St. John the Divine: "I am one tiny corpuscle in the body of Christ—and it is everything." We are that closely connected to the divine Source of Life. All too often we forget that we are created in the image, likeness, and potential of LoveConsciousness. We are spiritual presences with the capacity to be active radiations of Love, beneficial presences in the world.

To seek our particular place in the realm of LoveConsciousness is to go on a journey. Though it may be fraught with ego struggles that lead to pain, and even danger, the journey invites us to awaken to the fullness and joy of eternal life here and now, to recognize our gifts, and to live sharing them with others along the Way. As we become aware of our hunger to Awaken, we discover that we are already on a path with faith that we can walk along the same roads that Jesus walked. On this pilgrimage, we are wise to stop often for the true "pause that refreshes": silence, solitude, and prayer. For without them, we shall surely get distracted and find ourselves on detours that impede and delay our progress.

Our journey starts at birth when we are given a name. No matter how it was chosen, each name has importance and hidden power. "Now this is the word of the One who created you, the One who formed you; 'Fear not, for I have redeemed you, I have called you by name and you are mine'" (Isaiah 43:1). We have only to look at a few examples from Scripture to see that each name holds within it a meaning and an energetic power which asks something of us.

Mary, one of the most popular of all feminine names, was first recorded in the Bible as Mara: "Do not call me Naomi, ["my sweetness"], call me Mara, the bitter, for the Almighty has made my lot bitter" (Ruth 1:20). A derivative of myrrh, the precious, bitter ointment, the name Mary holds both of those qualities. Precious in our hearts, she can be a healing inspiration through the difficult, bitter times that season our lives. A nurturing name, Mary cares deeply for the safety of all her children, each one of us.

Martha as the "mistress" or "lady of the house" epitomizes the supreme pattern of homemaking. She is the practical one, who serves tirelessly. Sarah, whose name means "princess," was originally "Sarai, the quarrelsome," of the Bible. Her name was changed by God to Sarah who "laughed with joy" in her old age when her son was born. Though usually seen as sweet and loving, her name also denotes disruptions and dark shadows in her life.

We all know Peter, "a stone or rock," "on this Petra I will build my church." His name also points to "I am a man on a mission." Isaiah, who fought civic corruption in Judah (which, by its name, was meant to be a city "in praise" of God) seven hundred years before Jesus was born, means "salvation of God." Elizabeth, "oath of God" or "consecrated to God," indeed, as the mother of John the Baptist, lived fully into her name.

Our ancient forbearers knew the power of names and the alchemy of sound long ago. From the earliest times the name given to a child indicated the hopes, beliefs, or feelings of the parents, a quality of the person or of the circumstances—minor or momentous—connected with his or her birth. Most ancient and native peoples considered the name given to things or persons a basic energy having a special relationship to its bearer and calling forth the effective power of the individual. Like so many gifts of our forbearers, we now tend to live them out, more often than not, at an unconscious level.

Literature can often open the door to inner truths like this excerpt from *The Dean's Watch* by Elizabeth Goudge, which describes the power of being called by name:

> The Dean turned his gaze on the boy, his hand still absent-mindedly behind his ear, his sad eyes kindling. "Job Mooring," he repeated, "Job Mooring." The reiteration had an extraordinary strength; it gave back the lost identity and Job lifted his head and looked straight across the table at the Dean. It was years before he was to realize that a sense of identity is a gift of love, and only love can give it; but for the rest of his life he was to remember this moment when life began for him, real life, the life of the spirit and of genius which his world had foreshadowed.
>
> Years later, when he rose to make his first speech, he was suddenly back again in the city in the fen country, hearing his name spoken by the old Dean.[5]

God calls us by name, a gift of Love, and we belong to Love. Yet there are many forces in our society which would un-name us. The late Madeleine L'Engle in her book for children of all ages, *A Wind in the Door*, puts it clearly:

> "Progo! You said we are Namers. I still don't *know*: what is a Namer?"
>
> "I've *told* you. A Namer has to know who people are, and who they are meant to be. I don't know why I should be shocked to find Echthroi on your planet."
>
> "Why are they here?"
>
> "Echthroi are always about when there is war. They start all war; I think your mythology would call them fallen angels. War and hate are their business, and one of their chief weapons is un-Naming—making people not know who they are. If someone

knows who he is, really and truly knows, then he doesn't need to hate. That's why we still need Namers, because of places throughout the universe like your planet Earth. When everyone is really and truly Named, then the Echthroi will be vanquished."[6]

Yes, our society is filled with un-naming forces. More and more, we are referred to by numbers—Social Security, driver license, credit card, military, medical insurance. We get in lines at busy stores and are called our turn by numbers. One of the first things that happened in the Holocaust concentration camps, and that continues to happen in prisons today, is to be given a number. The prisoner, Jean Valjean, in *Les Miserables* is a powerful example of how demeaned and deadened one feels to be so unnamed. And the terrible danger is that when people begin to feel invisible, they will often either wither away or do something to get attention—more often than not, negatively, as one can observe any day in the media.

We can also be manipulated by names. For instance, are "smart bombs" that kill and maim really smart? Does a military operation dubbed "Trinity" really convey the meaning of Love that many people associate with it? And, who would think that the School of the Americas, still very much in operation in Virginia by a different, unrecognizable name, could be an institution for teaching individuals from many countries, including the United States, how to torture and to operate death squads to special training groups from many countries? Beware these names that disguise their use in order to make their deadly deeds less noticeable to an unsuspecting public.

What would it mean if we were to witness with visionary eyes, to extend love, forgiveness, assurance, and gratitude out to individuals in situations that seem beyond our own power to resolve: if we were to behold them through the eyes of Love? A friend recently shared that she joined a first, (for her) protest doing just that. As she left the protest feeling depressed, she noticed one woman sitting on the grass weeping in obvious anguish. My friend said that her action, her silent prayer protest, spoke louder than all the noisy, angry, sometimes violent protests being shouted. Our deeds do, indeed, speak volumes more than our words.

To attack others through words, thoughts, and/or actions is bound to return like a boomerang, exacerbating the negative energy. Just as fear begets fear, attack begets further attack. To birth peace, we must *become* the peace we seek; we must become peaceful in thought, word, and deed. For peace gives birth to peace, love gives birth to love and gratitude.

Names given in commercial ways by advertisers, by the military, by government programs imprint a certain quality or promise in our minds. These deceptions tend to key into people's yearnings and hopes, or spark a desire for more and more consumerism, whereas the big corporations and/or politicians get richer in their off-shore banks and seem to become more powerful. We must learn to call everything by its true name, especially the powers and principalities, the demons that would keep us dumbed down, inert, filled with fear, and apathetic! The need for individuals around the world to awaken has never been more crucial then today, now, in our time.

After facilitating a retreat group in a prayer-exercise to get in touch with the meaning and power of their own names, one woman in her mid-sixties came up to me and shared that she had always disliked her name. "Now," she said, "I can see that it is just exactly the right name for me. I have lived into its meaning without ever knowing it. I can really claim and enjoy my true name now for the first time."

Since our names are such an integral part of how we are known, we do well to notice them, to recognize how we relate to each part of our own distinctive appellation. We usually feel more comfortable being among those who know us by name. To speak another's name is an invitation to relate to that person in a particular way. And don't our hearts leap with joy when someone we love speaks our name? And, remember, those pangs of rejection we can feel when our name is spoken with derision or indifference. We may feel unseen when someone calls us by the wrong name, or forgets our name, that is unless we remember Who we are and Whose we are. For, the Beloved, who *is* Love, has called us by name and continues to call us by name.

The following prayer-exercise is a simple way to reverence the history of one's own unique name:

If you wish, set aside about fifteen minutes for a time of silence and solitude as you pray your name, pausing to ponder as indicated. Get comfortable. Just begin by slowly repeating your name to yourself a few times . . . Think of any nicknames you have had over the years. Imagine that you are a child again and hear your mother call you by name . . . your father . . . your sisters, brothers, or any special relative. Recall a few teachers along the way and hear them call you by name. Do the same with a few close friends over the years. Can you remember anyone calling you in a derogatory manner, name-calling, trying to unname you? How have you felt about your name over the years? If your name has changed in any way—through religious life, marriage, by choice—what difference has it made? How do you feel about your name now? Would you prefer a different name? What might it be? Imagine the Creator, the Source of your being, the Father, calling you by name. Imagine Jesus, as Friend and Loving Companion Presence, calling you by name. Imagine the Holy Spirit as a Dove whispering your name, calling you. Let Mary or Sophia as Wisdom speak your name. Finally, hear Gaia or the Earth itself, call your name. Now, take as much time as you need to ask for a word or words of wisdom, or perhaps to ask the question, "How can I (your name) best serve You?" . . . As you end this prayer, spend another few minutes in silence and solitude recalling that you are made in Love's image; Love calls you by name; you belong to Love; you are, in essence, Love.

Journaling about your name or sharing any feelings or insights with a friend is an added way of honoring and claiming the gift of your name. If you do not know the meaning of your name(s), they can usually be found in a what-to-name-the-baby book or, sometimes, in the back of large dictionaries.

My own life began as Nancy Elaine Crerie. Nancy ("grace") and Elaine ("Light") are simple, common, and I always liked them. Crerie posed problems. Spelled as people heard it pronounced, it ranged from Cleary, Quarrie or, worst of all, Queerie. My fourth grade teacher devastated me when she wrote in my autograph book: "Nancy Queerie, Queer Nancy, you're the girl that I fancy." Because I had unusual psychic experiences as a child and sometimes enjoyed the companionship of "unseen" friends, I already had a reputation of being considered odd by family and friends alike. In being named "queer" or, as I interpreted it, "crazy" by a beloved authority figure, I felt diminished and missed the benevolence of her intent. When I reread my autograph book sixty years later, I heard the teacher's words as lovesome, endearing, and playful. How vulnerable the young are to misinterpretation, betrayal, and hurt. We also can get a sense of the child we were in recalling our nicknames—some not always pleasant. Mine ranged from *nanny goat* to *pipsqueak, monkey, grasshopper, pesky, giggle-puss, string bean,* and *skinny bones.*

As a child growing up in the Episcopal Church, I long anticipated the time when I could be confirmed, which would open the door to the Mystery of receiving Communion. Eager to learn and understand the Catechism, I wanted to be fully prepared for this holy moment. Yet, the answer to the first question, "What is your name? My name is N or M," confounded me. So I kept nagging the teacher and my parents to explain what this meant—no way was my name going to be N or M. I was told in no uncertain terms by the teacher and my parents that it didn't matter what it meant, I was just to repeat it. Another way to get unnamed. To top it off, on the day of confirmation, the bishop blessed me as a "he." Didn't he see my pigtails? And instead of feeling "holy," and truly blessed as I had expected in a childlike way, I was simply confused, disappointed, and felt that I had somehow failed. Questioning authority seemed more fruitless than ever.

By the time I had come to appreciate the uniqueness of my family name, I was ready to marry and change it, happily assuming that was that. But years later, another more subtle name change emerged. I began to notice that the new friends I made called me Nan, a name I refused to be called growing up. Yet, it felt good. I accepted it. The full impact of this new name became clear one night at the dinner table when I was feeling out of sorts. One of the children, Pamela, now about eleven, observed, "I see

Nancy is back." Totally taken aback, I wanted to know what *that* meant. The response was simple. "Nancy is the old you—when you were fussy and sometimes even 'bitchy.' Nan is you now—most of the time. We all like her a whole lot better."

A final confirmation of this new name came at the end of my first—and most difficult—retreat. Not realizing that women were not openly welcomed at this particular retreat house, I arrived longing for silence, solitude, fasting, prayer, and Eucharist. Given a room near the garage and over the kitchen, I was told that the sisters were all away making their own retreat, and that I would be the only occupant in the building at night. I was denied Eucharist (not being Catholic) and was brought out of my silence more than I would have liked. Nevertheless, spending time with nature, reading Scripture, praying, and just being in silence and solitude seemed blessing enough.

Just before midnight on my last night at the retreat center, twice the light went on in the hallway outside my door. Each time, I went out and called to see who was there. No answer. I turned the light off and went back to bed. Then, about a half hour later, I heard eerie scraping sounds like chains being dragged in the supposedly empty room above me, and the light went back on. Once again, I called out. No answer. I turned the light off, put a chair against my door, which had no lock, and returned to bed. Then, just as I was dozing off, I suddenly felt a dark, almost palpable, presence in the room. I was afraid—to put it mildly. Then, I literally chose not to be afraid, to face fear head on. Knowing I was, theoretically at least, alone in the building, I spontaneously did what I had never done before: I called on the strong Name of Jesus. As long as I claimed the Name of Jesus, the room was peaceful and clear. As soon as I would begin to fall asleep, the dark presence returned. All night long I wrestled with that dark presence by calling silently from the depths of my heart on the strong Name of Jesus. Then at dawn, as church bells chimed in the distance, the room cleared and seemed now to pulsate with what I can only name as an energy of great Love. I heard within me a voice say: "You are simply Nan now, which means 'grace.' Claim your name and live into its meaning. You are not alone."

Although nothing momentous seemed to happen after the retreat, in retrospect, I recognized that once again the course of my life had changed. Love had called me to a whole new way of being; the Beloved had affirmed my new name, Nan, and had called me to a new life, a life of Service. The graces and gifts of Love are not given for ourselves alone; they are given to be shared as blessings in communion with our sisters and brothers around the world.

Many people today are tracing their genealogies, looking for the roots of their family trees. And, like the genealogies of Scripture and the history portrayed so powerfully in the "Roots" series on television, we do get a sense of where and what we have come from. Yet, we do not have to trace our family genes, revealing as that may be, to know Who and Whose we are. For we are each a blessed child of Love, called by name; we are each an individual consciousness, a unique presence, unconditionally loved by the Beloved, Who dwells within the Sacred Chapel of our heart. That we are made in the Divine image means that we are an integral part of the Source and we share in Divine Life. We are a dynamic part of the Divine Mystery.

We are, in fact, One with *all* our sisters and brothers, One in Being with the Source of All. We are born in and through LoveConsciousness destined to be co-creators in the Divine Plan for our planet. Yet, early on, we learn to follow the illusions of our own ego-stories. We seem separated from Love when we live in the fear-filled wilderness of our inner dramas that veil our true heritage as extenders of Love in the world, yet not of it. Jesus always encourages us to "choose Life." To choose Life is to ask for guidance, to listen in the Silence to the gentle voice of the Spirit, to take the roads to forgiveness, surrender, and unity, sharing our lives and resources with others. We begin by facing the wilderness illusions: the demons of fear, doubt, guilt, and sin that seem to enslave and separate us. Yet we soon discover that the demons fade away as the strength of Love is embraced. We are all together on this pilgrimage into Love.

3

The Road into the Wilderness

$\mathcal{T}$he road into the wilderness is where we come face to face with ourselves. Just before Jesus was led into the wilderness to face his own inner temptations so cleverly devised by Lucifer,[7] he was baptized by John, who having spent much of his life in the wilderness, really knew its potential and its many dangers. Yet, as he was to discover later, there is no wilderness as dangerous or deadly as that of an unruly, cruel heart bent on revenge or a weak, unprincipled authority figure willing to give in to peer pressure, as Herod did when he succumbed to the whims and wiles of his stepdaughter, who had been prompted by his wife to have John beheaded (Matthew 14:5–12).

What comes to mind when we hear the word "wilderness"? A dry, desolate, uninhabited, barren, unfertile, and uncultivated desert landscape, it is a home for wild and hungry, sometimes starving, animals, primeval, formless chaos, a lonely and fearful place or a space to be alone, away from crowds and the demands and distractions of society, a haven to listen deeply in silence and solitude, to be with the Divine Counselor, ever with us, ever available to hear our soul's concerns—even the unvoiced cries of the heart. So Jesus entered this wilderness road where John had been at home, having spent much of his life there eating simply and clothed with humility like the prophets before him.

And who is this strange man called John the Baptist? Does he have a relevant message for us in our day? We first meet John before his birth when Mary, pregnant with Jesus, came to visit Elizabeth. John leapt in his mother Elizabeth's womb in recognition of Jesus; could he have felt with her the imprint and impact of the Divine Spirit already at home in his cousin, Jesus, within Mary's womb? The next time we hear of John, he is preaching in the wilderness of Judea. In fulfillment of Isaiah's prophecy, he came as "the voice of one crying in the wilderness" calling those who would listen to awaken, to change, to repent and, thus, *to become more conscious*. And today his voice *must* resonate deeply within the hearts, souls, and divine-consciousness of us, individuals of hope, and hopefully, people of life-giving, loving action and forgiveness when faced with injustice of any kind.

Inviting others to repent and to join him, John began his ministry in preparation for the Blessed One who was to come. We may think of repentance as simply sorrow for past sins with new resolutions for the future. Yet far beyond that, repentance is a creative and affirming act that gives birth to new life and deepening integrity. While we can view "sin" as ego-illusions that *miss the mark,* a *metanoia*, means a complete turning around of the heart and mind, a recognition that all we experience as sin, guilt, fear is nothing but remnants of the past. To learn to live in the eternal *now* can lead us to a radical trust and spiritual revolution that changes everything, inspiring in us an evolving new purpose in life where we desire simply to Serve, to extend love and forgiveness, and to co-create with LoveConsciousness—ever in the world yet not of it.

John was a man of courage, not fearing to make enemies as he held to the truth. Calling the Pharisees and Sadduces "a brood of vipers" was far from politic. Walter Wink has suggested that John seemed to be saying to them, "Never mind your roots (with Abraham as your father), what are your fruits?" Alas, the Pharisees among us today seem pandemic. One has only to look at those in our society who presume to have it all made, those who bypass the poor, the oppressed, and those of a different race or creed. Regrettably, the Pharisee lurks in most of us. If we are wise, we will look within and root out all those self-righteous and hypocritical aspects of our egos, the areas where the letter of the law supersedes the Spirit of the law. And, that can be a path into the wilderness of our hearts.

To repent genuinely may be one of the most difficult things in the world to do. Yet, it is basic to all spiritual change and progress. For what does "to turn around" mean but to acknowledge as ego-illusions our pride, self-assurance, prestige, self-will, and to face all the subtler fear-illusions that lead to envy, anger, jealousy, sloth, and separation. How well we have been taught to defend against true repentance by blaming others, rationalizing, becoming emotional, personalizing, and intellectualizing—all the time projecting our fears, turning others into scapegoats!

When we recognize these defense mechanisms that we use as attack to quell our fears, we can see how doubly toxic they are, how they poison our lives and those of others. Fear is to our lives what plaque is to our arteries, building walls upon walls, clogging and stifling our well-being, unless and until we choose to eliminate them with love and care. Hidden in darkness, we unknowingly nourish our fears until they become so overwhelming they begin to rule our lives. In the Light of awakening and awareness, in the Love of forgiveness, our fears begin to disappear. As we face each fear, we will find our capacity to love increase proportionately. Perhaps all that holds us in the prison of fear at the core simply needs our compassion, our willingness to "risk" facing and forgiving ourselves through Love.

For, fear in whatever guise it may appear is most often a cry for help in a moment when we feel lost, alone, and helpless. Whenever it wells up, we do well to view it as an ego perception that seeks to veil Love: our true essence and home. Each time we catch a fear as one arises and we choose to face it, recalling *we are never alone* and calling on the Spirit of Truth for guidance and forgiveness, we lift the veil and glimpse the divine. We soon begin to experience the presence of authentic Love.

Now, if fear and all its companions have a debilitating energy within us, love, beauty, peace, joy, gentleness, and gratitude radiate life-giving energies. If fear with its manifestations and love's companions were on a menu each day, wouldn't our choice be a "no-brainer"? Yet, that *is* our life-or-death menu each day. Jesus was clear: "Choose life . . . life in abundance." To know that, ultimately, all that lurks in our shadow side as our fears diminish can become our greatest gifts, our deepest blessings. For we all carry untapped gold in the treasure house of Love *within* us.

Scripture reminds us, over and over, that Love is ever with us: "I am with you always—even to the end of time." I've been told that in one way or another we are reminded 366 times to "be not afraid," to "fear not," once for every day of the year including Leap year. To face our fears takes an act of will, a recognition that the ego's wiles are but habit-formed illusions, and to make the choice to call upon the Inner Voice of Love to guide us beyond ego ways of seeing to the Peace beyond what this world understands. As we are able to face this challenge, we begin to live in this world, yet without succumbing to its deceptive distractions and enticements. We become co-creators in the Service of Love similar to the energies of Love and Peace that St. Francis of Assisi embodied.

Luke's gospel has John preaching to special groups, including tax collectors and soldiers. John pointed to the need for reform, for practical foundations of sound, life-giving, moral behavior on which more-authentic spiritual structures of society could be built. Sound familiar? We do not need to look far to see how relevant this is for our times! Yet, we cannot afford to wait for the government and bureaucracies to respond to this immediate and critical call. We cannot allow ourselves to become overwhelmed by the magnitude of these terrible times. We must wake up and stay awake, lest we become hypnotized by the horrors of the daily news, or let the myriad distractions in our lives create boredom and apathy.

How does John live in you? Which of his qualities might you like to embody? What difference might John make in your life? Who have been and continue to be the lives and the voices in today's world that cry out in the wilderness? So many voices come to mind; so many voices have been silenced. Where would the world be now without Martin Luther King, Jr., Gandhi, the martyrs of Uganda and Central America, Mother Teresa, Jim Wallis, John Dear, Joan Chittister, Jean Prejean, Thomas Berry, Al Gore, and all those who protest and risk prison or even their lives on behalf of peace and justice and environmental renewal. How does your life cry out the Good News? Have you ever had the temptation to be a voice crying in the wilderness? Or is the temptation to be one of the silent, apathetic majority stronger? To face and forgive our ego-fear illusions is to become the peace and love our hearts yearn for.

The invitation to walk today with Jesus is not one of following a safe and comfortable path. To consciously say your *yes* may lead you to places you would rather not go. Yet, once *en route*, the journey is all that there is—it really *is* everything! Repentance is an ongoing journey in which we can recall our communal need for "washing" away the old. For, as we cleanse our hearts and minds of all that "misses the mark," of all that is not life-giving, we evolve into a deeper, more authentic life, into a greater capacity for Love, into a tapestry of life that celebrates diversity and Divinity in every aspect of Creation.

That John was known as "the Baptist" probably indicates the crux of his ministry, though John is clear that the baptism he offers is incomplete and provisional. "I baptize you with water for repentance, but the One who is coming after me is mightier than I, whose sandals I am not worthy to carry; that One will baptize you with the Holy Spirit and with fire" (Matthew 3:11). This was the central message of John's life: his every word and action pointed to Someone beyond, Someone who continues to come. We do well to ask ourselves from time to time, "Does my life carry a strong suggestion to others of Someone more powerful than I living within me?" We can name that Someone by whatever Divine Name resonates within our heart: Divine Guest, Loving Companion Presence, Beloved, Holy Wisdom, Love-Consciousness, Sophia, Jesus, Mary, Holy Spirit.

John baptized with water. What can water symbolize? At an exterior level, of course, pure water is a nurturing, cleansing, purifying and healing agent. Water is the essence of Life! Yet, in reference to the times, John was asking more than meets the eye when he baptized through immersion in the Jordan River. For baptism is where we receive the Water of Life, where we are plunged into the unseen Life of the Spirit ever at work in us. Water also symbolizes the feminine, the unconscious, which has been sorely repressed at all times including most cultures today. To accept baptism from John took a great act of trust. To go down under the water was to be taken symbolically into the dynamic, motivating feminine side of the personality and into the unconscious. Here the ego-self dies for that moment. Yet, when deeply accepted, diminishment of ego is to increase in Love and intuitive wisdom with enormous new potentialities: to be blessed with a deeper connection to one's inner being.

To understand the power of Baptism, of any true sacrament, takes a leap in faith. Yet this laying aside of the intellect and everyday mindset is difficult in societies where the mind rules so powerfully over the heart, where Love dwells. There is a cumulative power that one partakes of in each sacramental act. Centuries old, the rite of Baptism has welcomed myriad individuals from every nation, from every walk of life, to unite into the company of all those who aspire to develop toward authentic spiritual maturity within their particular faith. Each sacramental rite, when undertaken and received reverently in one's heart and spirit, imprints the individual with the brand of Love. When children are Baptized, a guideline for their future is bestowed as a loving parental promise for their care and upbringing with the community standing behind them. As an adult choosing Baptism with full consciousness, a commitment is made to move toward spiritual wholeness, to act justly with compassion, to witness to Love through one's life, to radiate Light in the world. This is no small decision. We join the countless pilgrims, who have aspired to walk the way of Love over the centuries.

Alan Jones, Dean of Grace Cathedral in San Francisco, emphasizes the importance of the sacrament of Baptism in an Epiphany letter to the congregation:

Baptism is the sacrament of conversion. It is an epiphany (a manifestation) of who we really are. Some of us were baptized as infants and knew nothing of what was going on in the beginning. This is just how it is for some of us with regard to conversion and transformation. We wonder how it all began and now we find ourselves living into the mystery of our baptism which happened before we had either knowledge or choice. God [Love] was there. God was with us. I experience a wild sense of gratitude that I was baptized as an infant. For others, baptism is a conscious choice, a deliberate decision, supported by the love and prayers of the community. It is a faster process—like running toward someone you love, whom you haven't seen for a long time. There's a marvelous urgency in preparing for baptism as an adult. It is time to live into the revelation by listening to the Great Stories of God's love for us, and by sharing experiences of transformation and conversion. One way or another, the baptized are called to be epiphanies to the world that God is here, God is with us.[8]

In essence, one accepts the invitation to become an ordinary contemplative, to move always toward wholeness and holiness. Paradoxically, as we are baptized by water, a Fire is ignited in our heart, the Fire of Love, that will hound us and haunt us no matter how far we try to run or how deeply we enmesh ourselves in the *busyness* of the world. As we are willing to face our fears and all that separates us from Love, this Fire will work in us, on us, and through us refining and transforming all that is dross within— our ignorance, weaknesses, doubts, and illusions—into dazzling, golden beams of Love.

Does this seem too much, too radical, too ideal? If so, it reflects how much easier it is to water down and dilute the tremendous transformative power and the boundless blessings of grace and unconditional love that are given as gift in the sacraments and through grace. This grace and love are the birthright of all, whatever the unique journey, wherever we are. No religion, denomination, class, dogma, or race are of concern in Divine Love. Everyone is equal in the eyes and heart of this Love.

Water, made up of two primal elements—oxygen and hydrogen—is the matrix in which all else exists, including our very bodies. Baptism by water is a symbol of life and death, burial and resurrection, a rite of initiation into a community of Life. So as we participate in this rite, we are called to see the whole world as sacrament, as blessing. Gratitude, deep inner peace, assurance, gentle joy and Love are appropriate responses as we share our lives with one another.

We cannot reflect on the meaning of water without taking a long, hard look at how the Pharisees in the world and the apathetic in us wantonly waste and pollute the Earth's waters. Big corporations and present governmental policies, or lack of them, to protect the environment, and refusal to comply with the world's standards add significantly to the disease, drought, famine, extinction of species, and overall pollution of the earth's atmosphere, water, and soil. Our mindless, and all-too-often unconscionable, choices are destroying and desecrating (i.e., taking away the sacredness from) our Earth home and destroying Gaia's ecosystem. Water's inner pathways through Earth's body can be likened to the blood coursing through our veins and arteries.

Can we bear to think of generations not yet born inhabiting a desolate wasteland devoid of its natural gifts, including Earth's wonders and beauty, that we could have saved? Beauty is a universal quality, an energy that extends itself. I learned this while refurbishing a grungy bathroom in the rectory of St. Agnes in Detroit, where I worked as a lay volunteer for four years in the mid 1980s. As a summer project I decided to begin what turned out to be a labor of love.

I trust that Father Ed would not have minded this aside: When I announced my plan to repair and paint the large kitchen over the summer while he was away, he said, "No way. I have a project for you." He may have thought I'd make it a bigger mess or never be able to complete it. When I shared my frustration with one of the sisters, she said with a smile, "You'd better learn now, it's sometimes easier to get forgiveness than permission." Since the kitchen was off-limits, I changed the "venue" starting on the grungiest room of all: the upstairs back bathroom. It turned out this was just the beginning. When Father Ed returned in the fall, he immediately gave me *carte blanche* to do all the refurbishing I could do.

Over the months of scraping, scrubbing, and painting the bathroom walls, I noted through the small window that the neighborhood could use a bit of upgrading, too. I imagined a roof being mended, windows and stairs being replaced, the old buildings on the property being cared for. These were gentle semi-conscious prayers for beauty, extended with the hope of renewal for the area.

Take on a new life, it did. Not only did all of the above occur; Bethune House on the property became a retreat house after volunteers refurbished it; the apartment on the property became Nazareth House, an alternative assisted-living home for parishioners run by Sister Marcella, who manifested her vision; the old run-down convent took on new life as a charismatic group found volunteers to renovate it completely. Beauty, not me, had spread her energy in ways that I could never at that time have imagined. I share this as an invitation to begin seeing the world with new eyes, eyes that see beyond the outer scene to what will manifest with Beauty's vision. Nicolas Roerich[9], a Russian mystic and artist, tells us that Beauty, which is universal, can save the world!

Nature is another form of Beauty, although sometimes what Yeats called a "terrible beauty." We cannot afford to lose all the gifts that Beauty bestows on us. Never has forgiveness, repentance, and right action been more crucial. Who will do it if not each one of us? Let us baptize the world with our love, with Love!

Each time we are present at a new Baptism, we are invited to remember how interconnected and interdependent our lives and bodies are with water and air, with the earth and its gifts and resources, with one another. Baptism calls us to make Love conscious in our lives, to give praise and thanks for the blessings of the earth and to share ourselves, our unique consciousnesses and gifts, even as we live as One with the gracious Giver of breath and life.

Sometimes a creative use of our imagination, that gift unique to humankind, as far as we know, is to travel back in time. So, if you wish (pausing at each break):

Just imagine yourself back about two thousand years ago. Hot and dusty from walking a long ways, you follow a great crowd to the edge of the Jordan River. Notice the variety of trees and shrubs along the river's edge. John, whom you have come to hear, breaks your reverie shouting, "Prepare the way for the One Who is to come bearing the beams of Love and Life." What does this mean? How do we respond to these words? Does he really mean you, when he cries out? Watch John as he enters the water, as he wades out and turns to the crowd, raising his arms and voice, he is crying out over and over, "Repent all of you, repent. Prepare yourself for the One who is coming." How is your heart prepared for Love's indwelling presence? Are you ready? Now, people are making their way through the crowd and into the water. Feel the growing intensity. One by one, John immerses them, brings them up, and they merge back into the crowd. How do they seem as they emerge from the water? Move closer to the water's edge. Will you step into the water or not? And then, as if in answer to an unvoiced prayer, you remember a whole area in your life that is hidden and not life-giving. Do you want to repent, to ask for forgiveness, and change? (Here, if you wish, take time to see if this is true in your own life. If so, reflect and pray about it and then just carry it with you as you get to the water's edge.) Suddenly, you begin to move toward John. When your turn comes to be immersed, John takes you into his dark, ample arms and lowers you into the waters, into the depths . . . and then back to the surface where you emerge dripping. As your eyes begin to focus, you see that John is looking with expectant eyes at a man making his way through the crowd. You begin to walk toward this newcomer and feel a radiance of Love envelop you. Somehow, you know the others standing around must feel it, too. Just bask in the cocoon of Love enveloping you as you gaze into the eyes of this man someone nearby has called Jesus. Do you feel any different? Imagine Jesus putting his healing hand of Light on your head and blessing you. Hear inwardly a promise that you can become freer to live into the fullness of the unique individual you were born to be.

A simple prayer-exercise, to be sure. Yet, our thoughts and imagination are, in fact, like prayers. While all negative thoughts bear an energy that has self-fulfilling results, something new can be born in us through imagination, forgiveness, and heartfelt thoughts. Our baptism is a new beginning, a pilgrimage, a place where we have arrived and a place we are always moving toward. Our baptism is the beginning of a journey where we are to perceive and experience the world in a new way. We are to live in loving relationship with our family, our friends and neighbors, strangers—and, yes, even with those who seem to be our enemies. The change to which we are called is a lifelong process of walking step-by-step through our fears and darkness into the light of God's mercy until every part of us—our bodies, minds, heart, personality, senses and will—has been re-created by Love.

In his book, *Flute Solo: Reflections of a Trappist Hermit*, Matthew Kelty reminds us of how something as simple and commonplace as rain can symbolically be an opportunity that reawakens us to the lifelong invitation to renew the power of our baptism, to rediscover the joy and spontaneity of a child, and to experience nature's on-going baptisms:

Water is always an invitation to immersion [for me], an immersion with a quality of totality, since it would accept all of me, as I am. Some primal urge invites me to return from whence I came.

At times I have done so. There is some special delight in simply walking into a stream, stepping into a lake. The child's delight in a puddle is my adult's in the sea.

No rain falls that I do not at once hear in the sound of the falling water an invitation to come to the wedding. It is rare that I do not answer. A walk in an evening rain in any setting is to walk in the midst of God's loving attention to the earth, and, like a baptism, is no simple washing, but a communication of life. When you hurry in out of the rain, I hurry out into it, for it is a sign that all is well, that God loves, that good is to follow. If suffering a doubt, I find myself looking to rain as a good omen. And in rain, I always hear singing, wordless chant rising and falling.

When rain turns to ice and snow, I declare a holiday. I could as easily resist as stay at a desk with a parade going by in the street below. I cannot hide the delight that then possesses my heart. Only God could have surprised rain with such a change of dress as ice and snow.

Most people love rain, water. Snow charms all your hearts. Only when you get older and bones begin to feel dampness, when snow becomes a traffic problem and a burden in the driveway, when wet means dirt—then the poetry takes flight and God's love play is not noted.

But I am still a child and have no desire to take on the ways of death. I shall continue to heed water's invitation, the call of the rain. We are in love and lovers are a little mad.[10]

"Lovers are a little mad." We are all invited to play in the rain, to become lovers of life like children splashing at the ocean's edge. These are some beautiful images of baptism. How many of us are still in touch with the Divine Child within us? Who among us recognizes rain and snow, and wind and clouds as poetry? And, where are the lovers who play in creation? I know a few rare souls who dance the Dance, yet regrettably, not many. Is it too much to believe that our baptism is an invitation to participate in the Cosmic Dance?

And then Jesus came from Galilee to the Jordan to be baptized by John. And when Jesus was baptized, he went up immediately from the water, and behold, the heavens were opened and he saw the Spirit of God descending like a dove and alighting on him; and lo, a voice from heaven saying, "This is my beloved Son, with whom I am well pleased" (Matthew 3:16–17).

What does it mean, we might ask, that Jesus came to John to be baptized? Perhaps, besides fulfilling "all righteousness," Jesus came to support John in his ministry. Perhaps, Jesus intuited the coming days in the wilderness and wondered about the possibility of choosing to avoid the mission for which he had come. Or, since Jesus never thought of himself in isolation, perhaps he was baptized into the people's need for a cleansing of the heart in order to express the urgency of commitment to the realm of Love. Jesus was well aware that Israel as a nation needed to repent, just as we, today, are a nation in dire need of repentance. And, Jesus must have been aware that a mission was to be placed on him. "Here is my servant whom I uphold, my chosen one in whom my soul delights. I have sent my Spirit upon him, he will bring fair judgment to the nations" (Isaiah 42:1).

At the baptism of Jesus, the Holy Spirit breaks through. LoveConsciousness was ordained by the Creator, Life of all life, with the mission to become a mediator between heaven and earth, between individual and universal consciousness, with all the pain that would entail. Just as the heavens were rent at Jesus' baptism to bring forth the Spirit, so at the Cross would the heavens again be rended to receive back the Spirit of LoveConsciousness, now manifest as the Christ Consciousness.

Jesus began his mission with baptism by water just as we, too, can be baptized with water. Our baptism, whether within a church or as a choice to share with friends in nature, this sacrament of new beginnings, symbolizes the death and transformation of the ego false self, an emptying out so that we can be filled with the Holy Spirit in the baptism by Fire. While John's baptism implies righteous fear, baptism by fire and the Spirit implies redeeming love, new life, and resurrection of the spiritual self, a rebirth by Divine Love, Light, and Power. We share in the life and vitality of a Love that enables us to lead a new and more conscious life. We are invited to become co-workers, co-creators, and co-lovers, companions with and through LoveConsciousness all along our pilgrimage.

What part of this journey can you see yourself taking? What is the meaning of baptism in your life? Can you accept the purposes to which Love calls you? How can you allow your life to be set in the larger framework of Love's will? Can you imagine the Spirit saying to you, "This is my beloved daughter, my beloved son, with whom I am well pleased?"

Although baptism is a public declaration by the community, all peoples are children of the earth, children of the Source of Life that created the universe. Baptism acknowledges a Presence working within us at the deepest part of our being throughout our lives, One that leads us toward eternal life. John reminds us today, just as he witnessed to the crowds of his day, by telling us that when we are baptized in the name of LoveConsciousness for the forgiveness of all that separates us from the Source of Life, we will receive the gift of the Divine Fire, the Fire that hones us into new Life. This promise is as true today as it was then. What we do with this great gift of grace is up to us!

All through our lives, we do well to confess our faith over and over in order to preserve Love's sacramental gift. We need to keep telling our story to remember that we are called to become what we already are. We are made in the image of Love and we are made to radiate Love and to be Light for the world. We have the capacity to be beneficial presences, which Dr. Thomas Hora[11] in his books and teaching describes in this way: "A beneficial presence in the world is a channel through whom the goodness of Love expresses Itself."

Baptism is always a new beginning inviting us, prodding us, leading or driving us to walk the roads that Jesus walked, knowing that we are not alone. We have a faith community, we belong, we have a family. We have the indwelling Divine Guest. And the Spirit pursues and calls us to become more conscious, to cultivate a heart of unlimited compassion and love toward *all* of Creation, to become all that we can be. Thus, through Love's grace, we can be a blessing for others and for our Earth home. We receive abundant blessings as we consciously choose to follow the Way, the Truth, and the Life of Love.

4

The Road through the Wilderness

In the wilderness or desert, we are more vulnerable to the Spirit working in us. Here, we cannot hide from areas of darkness we've been unaware of or have kept in the closet; now, we are forced or we can choose to meet our selves, our senses, our mind, and our emotions face-to-face. Be it our fear or fear's companions: guilt, doubt, disappointment, feelings of emptiness, loneliness, rejection, or abandonment, be it our unfulfilled joy, dreams, gifts, hopes, or purpose, or, be it some act or decision we sense is not for our highest good, we are faced with the mirror of our soul's inner landscape. When we carry the strong arm of faith and stop often to be nourished by times of prayer, spiritual reading, solitude, and silence as Jesus did throughout his life, the perils of the journey through the wilderness can become a grace with life-giving changes. And more often than not, we recognize the One who is ever with us, who has already led the way, who is as close to us as our next breath, waiting—always waiting—to embrace us with tender and merciful love.

The wilderness can often be a humbling road where we see how poor, judgmental, fragmented, structured, complex, and bi-ased we've become. Our hearts are tested and we must acknowl-edge how far we've strayed from the Realm of Love. Yet, "*blessed* are the poor, the simple, in spirit, for theirs is the *kindom* of heaven." In our humility and poverty, we feel a sense of separation from the One who is always calling us. In the *busyness* of our lives, we can easily forget that Love is the essence and source of our life and being. To be mindful of Love or our own holiness (which we often tend to deny) in our relating, working, thinking, praying, in every aspect of our life is energy-effective, cost-effective, and socially-effective. Love is the energy of the world, despite outward appearances. Love is simple and can cut through problems, enmity, chaos by getting to the root of things, the bottom line. We are created by Love, for Love: we are Love and we are holy in our deepest core. We are closer than we can imagine to redeeming, forgiving Love, to the gentle, patient Lover who never gives up on us.

Wise are those who consciously choose to walk into the wilderness by taking "desert days," those crucial times when all else is set aside so that the voice of the Spirit's indwelling Presence within the silence of our hearts might be heard! To calendar in a "desert day" or week simply to *be* alone with the Lover of your heart and soul, to bask in silence, to read life-giving, spiritually nourishing materials, to fast or eat simply is a way of saying *yes* to the Source of all life. Moreover, it is to get de-stressed, lower blood pressure, and to receive Love's energy awakening more fully within. Mind-fasting could be the most needed element of time apart. To drop our concerns, problems, obsessive thought patterns opens the door for all that wants to surface to come forth. Then, emptied, we are freer to participate in and with One Mind:[12] LoveConsciousness. Nature walks or simply sitting and observing (away from technology with all its disruptions and distractions) is almost always a healing balm during those days.

Jesus is the model for walking with us through the desert. For, after being baptized, "Jesus was led up by the Spirit into the wilderness *to be tempted* by the devil. He fasted forty days and forty nights and, afterward, he was hungry" (Matthew 4:1–2). According to Mark's gospel, the Spirit *drove* Jesus out into the wilderness: quite a sharp contrast to being called "my beloved Son!" One might wonder that the Spirit itself did not test Jesus, that the Spirit was aware of what was to happen. There seems to be some connection in the discernment process between the

Spirit and Satan. For, one remembers God's permission given to Satan for the testing of Job. And, we cannot help but reflect on the forty years of Israel in the desert—a time of temptation and failure for Israel. No wonder Jesus' prayer that we have offered over the centuries implores the Spirit to "Lead us not into temptation, but deliver us from evil."

So, the tempter came and said to Jesus, "*If* you are the Son of God, command these stones to become loaves of bread" (Matthew 4:3). (Luke uses the term *devil*, a subtle difference.) Whereas the tempter performs a function, the devil is often considered the personification of evil who we blame for leading us off the path. "The devil made me do it." The tempter starts the seduction with that little *if* word that has been the source of so much anguish. What does *if* do but create doubt and invite conflict. How many times in our own lives have we fallen into the hands of the *if only* syndrome. When you hear *if* on your pilgrimage, beware of temptation.

What would it mean to turn stones into bread? (John the Baptist had told the Pharisees and Sadduces when they came to be baptized that God could turn stones into the children of Abraham.) To begin with, Jesus must have been hungry. At a personal level, he could prove his power by feeding himself had he so chosen. Beyond that, Jesus was very much aware of how the Roman taxes were creating economic chaos for the poor. So, the tempter is inviting Jesus to provide for the people—to feed the poor and hungry—through the use of miraculous power.

Now Jesus never denied the ordinary needs of people, for we know how he showed compassion for the hungry crowds by multiplying bread and fish so that they could eat; and, he changed water into wine so the wedding guests could celebrate. To feed the hungry would be good and the people were awaiting the One who would come and take care of their needs, just as God had met their needs with manna in the desert. How "comforting" it has been for two thousand years to expect Jesus to do *it* for us, rather than living fully into our own potential as co-creators with Love.

But Jesus answered, "It is written, 'Let us not live by bread alone, but by every word that proceeds from the mouth of God.'" (Deuteronomy 8:3). So notwithstanding the Israelites yearning for a Messiah who would meet their desires and expectations *now*, for, after all, they had been waiting for so long, Jesus' answer puts those needs as secondary to LoveConsciousness, the Word of God. Recognizing that the poor will always be with us, Jesus claims and proclaims always that which is most life-giving. The implied message is that those who live in harmony, in unity with LoveConsciousness, will be *inwardly* at peace even as the walls of their hearts are broken and blessed. Then, they will be sent out to those in need, sometimes to places that they would rather not go. Yet, they will be empowered to live in a more responsible, grateful, life-giving, and nurturing way. They will see the needs of others and respond as they follow Love's Way, Truth, and Life.

In saying *no* to the tempter, Jesus says *no* to all who look to him to gratify their own desires. Rather, we are invited to follow the road that leads to forgiveness and making the decision to ask the Spirit of Truth to help us, to let go of all the ego illusions that separate us from Love and to claim the divine ideals that lead to eternal life. That Jesus made this clear in his ministry can be seen in John's gospel. When the multitudes were searching for him, Jesus said: "In all truth I tell you, you are looking for me not because you have seen the signs, but because you had all the bread you wanted to eat. Do not work for food that goes bad, but work for Food that endures for eternal life" (John 6:26–27). And when they asked for that bread, Jesus answered them, saying, "I am the Bread of Life. The one who comes to me will never hunger." The one who regularly follows Jesus' example in the "desert of soul-searching" with times of prayer, solitude, and silence is likely to find new life *in* the world yet not *of* it. Abundant life as we become bread of life for others.

We all have had the temptation to pray fervently for what we want here and now feeling certain it will be best for us. Therefore, how could it not be God's Will? Here, we are not much different from the multitudes that followed Jesus for what they could get.

A dream clarified for me just such a temptation, probably, because I insisted on denying its possible ramifications over and over again while "awake" despite the red flags. Having finally asked for a dream to help my discernment process, I dreamed. . . .

I was hanging by my fingertips from the rooftop of a very tall skyscraper. I was relieved to hear someone coming to help—or, so I thought. When I looked up, the devil stood there dressed in full array—cloven hooves, pitchfork, and horns. Smiling at me, he said, "I know your heart's desire; I will give you what you want—if only." I did not want anything to do with the devil and let him know it. He began to taunt me, saying, "I'll give you all that you have been praying for—everything—if only," as he kicked at my fingertips with his hooves. I struggled mightily, not daring to let go, which seemed too much like suicide, selling my soul, and giving him my power, yet not intending to give in to his seductive offering. When it became apparent that I would not accept his "invitation," he gave my fingers a hard kick of frustration. I fell. Falling . . . falling . . . and suddenly, a black cloud of letters floated under me and gently brought me back to earth. I was saved by the words that the letters formed: *You shall know the truth, and the truth shall set you free* (John 8:32).

This really got my attention. This quotation was the first Bible verse I learned as a child, a verse that I have carried in my heart as a lodestar all of my life. Indeed, in bringing a real and much-desired temptation out of denial, I could no longer hide from the truth. And, thanks be to all that is Holy, I did not get my heart's desire, which, in retrospect, was clearly not in anyone's best interest. So I asked forgiveness for myself and all involved; then, I abandoned myself and my futile, unrealistic dreams into Love's hands. What I learned from the tempter helped me to see the importance of clarifying my priorities, naming the temptation, and asking deep within my inner being for help. I could also recognize that Lucifer, who had shined light into my darkness, had done his work well.

The tempter, showing that he, too, knew Scripture, took Jesus to the holy city, Jerusalem, and set him on the pinnacle of the temple saying, "*If* you are the Son of God, throw yourself down; for it is written, 'God will give his angels charge of you' and 'in their hands they will bear you up, lest you strike your foot against a stone'" (Psalm 91:11–12). Besides attempting once again to create doubt with his opening *if,* what is the tempter up to here? What could be accomplished from leaping from the Temple of Jerusalem for all to see? Who would be drawn to this kind of Messiah? Jesus does not succumb to the use of miraculous power to give evidence by providing a great and spectacular "sign." To compel the multitudes to believe through such a crowd-pleasing display was to tempt God—another subtle ruse of the devil.

People are in awe of power; and though its terrible beauty and magnetism often create fear, power is also difficult to resist. To give in to this temptation would mean instant "success" with thousands of followers, but would give birth to a totally different mission than that to which Jesus was being called. Once again, Jesus' response is that of the feminine: a seemingly defenseless, yet hidden power which leads to authentic, life-giving results.

The following quotation was sent to me many years ago; I do not remember who shared it or its source. I offer it as an example of how dangerous the irresponsible acceptance of one of the tempter's ploys to power can be when an individual with authority succumbs.

> Beware the leader who bangs the drums of war in order to whip the citizenry into a patriotic fervor, for patriotism is indeed a double-edged sword. It both emboldens the blood, just as it narrows the mind. And when the drums of war have reached a fever pitch and the blood boils with hate and the mind has closed, the leader will have no need in seizing the rights of the citizenry. Rather, the citizenry, infused with fear and blinded by patriotism, will offer up all their rights unto the leader, and gladly so. How do I know? For this is what I have done. And I am Caesar.

Another illustration of our need to awaken, to be not afraid, and to be ever vigilant on our journey.

Once again, Jesus answered Scripture with Scripture: Again it is written, "You shall not tempt the Lord your God" (Deuteronomy 6:16). Jesus reminds the tempter that he knows what happens to those who seek signs such as the people coerced Moses to do. By producing the waters of Meribah from the rock, Moses lost his right to lead the people into the Promised Land.

All through his ministry Jesus sought to remain out of the limelight, telling those who were helped and cured, "Do not tell anybody;" "Do not go into town;" "Tell no one." To Peter he had to say, get behind me, Satan! Because the way you think is not Love's way but the world's (Mark 8:33). How few understood. Those closest to him tried to influence him. His brothers told him to leave this place and go to Judea, so that his disciples, too, could see the works he was doing. No one who wants to be publicly known acts in secret. If this is what you are doing, you should reveal yourself to the world. Not even his brothers had faith in him (John 7:1–5).

So the tempter took Jesus to Jerusalem to offer him the city, the Temple, the "rock-star" role. The people wanted a high Priest, a miracle worker, someone to work wonders on their behalf. They expected the Messiah to come in glory riding in with hosts of angels and armies—surely something more spectacular than a baby born in a stable, a humble carpenter. Jesus says, *no*: this is not how God, LoveConsciousness, is revealed.

At the end of his mission, Jesus goes again to Jerusalem, where he is condemned to die, seemingly a failure. And no one understood. If we allow Jesus to point the way, our journey is bound to lead us to Jerusalem, the true Jerusalem of our hearts, where all prophetic hope will be perfectly fulfilled. How difficult it is to recognize that salvation comes humbly, simply, by way of faith in our Oneness with Love, with the guidance of the Counselor, by choosing the way of forgiveness, and by learning that we are *all* in this journey into Love together. Yet, how few of us realize in our chaotic, Internet, media-oriented times any value in long pauses for silence and solitude, pauses to fast both the body and mind, pauses to reflect on the many ways LoveConsciousness is ever-present to us, ready to guide us to lives of peace and joy.

The Realm of Love can only come one person at a time. The route to this realm has been well paved by Jesus and Teachers from many faiths, the community of saints before us, prophets of all time including those who speak for peace, love, and justice today, the growing number of spiritual centers, as well as the many teaching courses available on tape, in retreats, and books that lead to right action like *A Course in Miracles*.[13]

What meaning does Jesus' temptation to have great power over others have for us unless we look within to discover our own weaknesses, pride, and yearning to be first, to be on top, to be in control? Working in us and with us, Jesus' life shows us the way and, as loving companion Presence, we have a Friend forever. We are given all we need to know ourselves as *light of the world* living in the peace of Love-with-us always. And does this not call us as a nation to reflect on our way of life, our foreign policies, our materialism, the way we treat the poor at home and in the world, especially the third-world countries where refuge "cities" filled with disease and famine take the lives of untold individuals—primarily the elderly, women, and children?

The work of Satan can be seen and heard minute by minute through the media. What a welcome relief when we hear some good news of the day! Yet, the good news is not a big money-maker. It doesn't create an adrenalin rush or fully distract us from the "daily grind." Just the fact that so many people are stressed and consider their work a daily grind speaks loudly to our lives being way out of kilter, out of balance. The world needs more witnesses whose lives reflect LoveConsciousness guiding our lives today in order to keep the Good News relevant. We can authentically witness most effectively through our lives and life experiences; for, words often tend to separate, distort, and con-fuse our journey rather than to unite us to Love. Moments spent in the Silence throughout the day can speak far more eloquently than words. Silence can be a restorative pause that helps us to reorient our priorities, center us, and guide us to where we are most needed.

In this spirit, I share incidents of my pilgrimage simply as an invitation to you to pause from time to time to get an overview of your life with all its temptations and joys, to share how Love is threading its way through your life story. This particular temptation reminds me of an event that turned from a minor "disaster" into a blessing. First, the background:

> One evening, when our family—Ray, the five children, assorted pets and I—was moving from California to Maryland, we stopped for an early dinner. Needless to say, having been cramped in the station wagon all day, the children were restless and impatient. Service was slow. After a long wait and no food, our youngest son, Jim, who was a year-and-a-half, suddenly and without warning let out a blood-curdling scream of frustration. His timing could not have been worse. The waitress had just arrived behind Jim's highchair holding a tray of filled glasses above her head just as he screamed. And, yes, startled, she dropped the tray.
>
> The combination of the noise of the glass breaking and the other children all blaming Jim overwhelmed him. He just went limp and slid through the highchair to the floor. It took a long time to bring him back from his coma-like condition; it seemed as if he just wanted to disappear. And for almost a decade after that traumatic event, whenever Jim spilled anything—and, because it was a *big* and pretty much *unconscious* fear, it happened regularly—his reaction was always the same: instantly going limp and "disappearing."

One day years later, we were expecting "important" guests for dinner. I had stopped to admire the kitchen floor, having just washed and waxed it, when Jim, who was now in fifth grade, came in from school. As he opened a half-gallon container of milk, it slipped from his hands. As I watched the milk flow over my shiny floor and under the refrigerator, the strong temptation was to yell at Jim. I was riding on a high-horse of pride hoping to impress the guests due to arrive within an hour or so. In that moment, the flowing milk seemed to be spoiling my vain efforts. In fact, I had a major disproportionate ego-desire to impress the expected company by being a five-star "super hostess."

The temptation to explode became so strong, I found myself moving quickly toward Jim in great frustration. But instead of berating him, the Divine Guest within me took over. Suddenly, my heart was filled with compassion as Jim began to "disappear."

I quickly hugged him and held him up in my arms saying with a firmness foreign to my usual way-of-being, "I love you, Jim, I love you. It's okay to spill. But when you do, it is your responsibility to clean it up. I'll help you this time, but from now on, it's up to you." And we cleaned it up together.

What had happened? I believe that had I not been prepared for that very moment through a mother's prayers of placing that particular concern in Love's hands over the years, I might very well have missed a beautiful opportunity to *be* there for Jim, to allow Love to break through my pride and impatience and creating a catalyst for Jim to heal. Never again did he "disappear" and rarely did he ever again spill anything. And gratefully, my priorities were realigned; I grew in strength, balance, and understanding: the fruits of saying *no* to that reactive temptation and of having spent time in silence and prayer. My friends used to laugh when I talked about "being in harmony with the universe." Yet, that is only another way of expressing the feeling of being at-one-with LoveConsciousness.

Compared to Jesus, our temptations may seem puny and trivial. Yet, they are grist for the mill, the daily trials that hone us. Love is a refining Fire; yet we are usually singed little by little with great and tender mercy.

Again, the devil took Jesus to a very high mountain, and *showed him* all the nations of the world and the glory of them, saying "All these I will give you *if* you will fall down and worship me." Then Jesus responded, "Begone, Satan! For it is written, 'You shall worship the Lord your God, and God only shall you serve'" (Mt. 3:13).

Since the "*if* you are the Son of God" did not work, the devil changed strategy and "showed" Jesus an easy way to get authority, political power, and glory—and, only then, slipped in the "*if*." The people were expecting, yearning for, a divine king. And Lucifer is offering that power to Jesus on a platter, so to speak. What a temptation it must have been for Jesus to think how easily Love's glory could be won, how peace could reign under the leadership of the Son of God. Then the words from Deuteronomy must have come to mind. "Yahweh, your God, is the one you must fear, him alone you must serve, his is the name by which you must swear." So Jesus *named* the tempter by crying out, "Begone, Satan."

Jesus may have been impatient with this process by now. But, more than that, there is tremendous power in naming our adversaries, the false gods that would entice us to be less than our birthright. In naming Satan with an injunction to leave, Jesus claims the authentic power of the One whose Way is to be reverenced, Who is to be served, and to Whom he will be faithful. Jesus' mission is clearly not going to be what the populace wanted, hoped for, or thought they needed. He has "disidentified" with the expected roles of prophet, priest, and king. Jesus now stands alone to await the Will of the One who sent him. In effect, Jesus has said a resounding "No" to following yesterday's will of God, recognizing that God is always creating anew and inviting us to awaken to our Oneness in LoveConsciousness, as co-creators and extenders of Love.

Each of the devil's temptations is aimed at hooking into our ego-self. In saying "no," Jesus' responses to the tempter are authentic models for de-creating the power of the false ego, the carrier of all our insecurities that feed on fear. This releases energy for transformation to more mature and life-giving decisions, for re-creation, for increasing our Love quotient.

We know what happens to us when we do not go into the wilderness to confront our ego's demons. Usually, we get stuck, we become sticks-in-the-mud, hanging on to old roles and ways-of-being that we have long outgrown, but that we are afraid to change. This becomes a choice not to grow and mature spiritually or to become fully alive to our inner potential. We take the "easy" road of remaining in the closet, like some worn garment we can't bear to part with. We are blessed as we discover that *as* we face our fears, temptations, and weaknesses, we find love filling us and energizing us into the Life that Jesus' entire life modeled. Jesus didn't live and die fully so we wouldn't have to. His life is an unparalleled gift that invites each one of us to live into the fullest individual (your name) in every way that we can, wherever and whatever our situation in this life may be.

How regrettable it is when parents rear their children to be extensions of themselves, when they clutch at their children's lives as preservers of their own ego needs, when they continue to live vicariously through their children's work, marriages, friends, and grandchildren. (This is, of course, not to disavow the beauty and joy of appropriately sharing our lives with them.) And what is as impotent as those whose entire lives unconsciously or like robots revolve around their role or position in work and society? Blessed are you whose life, work, and leisure make your heart sing and brings fulfillment and joy. And happy are you who choose to walk the road that Jesus took into the wilderness with all its struggles and commitment and to attend the process by which you awaken in LoveConsciousness by surrendering to Love's Will. Here you abandon yourself into the hands of Love to face your fears, to discern how you can best serve Love.

What would it mean if the churches and other institutions were to choose this road? So many seem to be just wandering in the wilderness wondering why LoveConsciousness seems not to hear the prayers to heal all the problems that beset them. Could it be that we are hanging on to yesterday's will of God? Could it be that the religious, social, political, and economic institutions have succumbed to one of the tempters greatest dangers—to remain static, to trust worldly "powers," to hold back growth and new life in the Spirit?

Still, "The Spirit broods over us with, ah, such bright wings!" wrote the poet Gerald Manley Hopkins. Yet how open are we as a people to receive and live the New Creation awaiting birth? We claim to deplore abortion, war, and all that leads to unnecessary and untimely death in the flowering of life. Yet, what hypocrites we are as we apply the death penalty, declare war, and manufacture all the murdering, maiming instruments of death. And, how often do we abort and kill the hopes and plans of the Spirit for our own lives today?

Perhaps the most powerful weapons the tempter uses are apathy and feelings of powerlessness. We become the ones who say, "if only" this or that would happen in our ever-busier lives, in our red-tape, paper-driven institutions, in too many insensitive, greedy corporations, in our power-hungry, increasingly secretive politics, our noisy, complex, manipulative, materialistic world. Not a pretty, nor a petty, indictment!

What will it take for we the people, who *are* the church and society, who *are* the government with its myriad departments, who *are* the only ones who can put a stop to the irresponsible mess we've allowed to fester into an Earth-cancer? How are we to end our madness and to heal our raped and razed earth, our increasingly fragile ecosystem, our broken, out-of-control financial system, our outdated, old fashioned energy usage, our dysfunctional health and educational systems, and even our infrastructures that cry for a creative, secure *metanoia*, a massive turn around?

We *must* Awaken and join with the growing numbers of networks of concerned citizens who are working for and serving the Source of all Life for the healing, renewal, and blessing of Creation, whose tapestry of beauty encompasses every individual in every aspect of life. One by one, we can do it. Jesus' life points the way! We forget that we are never alone, that inspiration, strength, and commitment come out of the wilderness, desert days of silence and prayer in solitude, where we can hear the Voice of the Spirit. When we consciously *choose* to spend more time alone or in dialogue with those responsible for making crucial decisions on behalf of others, when we refrain from reactive choices, then, we can respond by allowing the Creative Muse to speak to us, we can pray with an intensity that mirrors the woman importuning the judge in Scripture (Luke 18:3). We can sow our seeds in truly fertile soil, unlike seed strewn among rocky and thorny soil (Mt. 13:1–9).

After wrestling with the tempter for forty days and nights, Jesus chose for all time to offer forgiveness and love as a way for individuals to disidentify from their ego illusions in order to serve in harmony and oneness with the Creator. And when this long debate was over and the tempter gone, the angels came and ministered to Jesus.

"And when the devil left him, the angels came and ministered to Jesus." We really deprive ourselves of so much guidance, comfort, and company when we ignore the angelic presences in our lives in both realms: heaven and earth. It is a rare day when I do not acknowledge and express gratitude for many moments of insight and help from "my" angels, always with a companioning sense of angels with me. Who are the angels in our lives? Can you recall a time of being ministered to by an angel? Are you aware that during our spiritual struggles, like Jesus' time in the wilderness, angels avail us of re-creative energy—and more.

In our day, society as a whole tends not to give much credence to angels—except as trimming for the Christmas tree and as messengers of the past. We do both the angelic realm and ourselves a great disservice. For, what we do not believe in, we cannot easily experience. Recently, what seemed to arise as an angelic fad has become a business, a big Hint of what is possible, and a growing awareness and appreciation for their ministering, co-creative relationship with us. Many individuals simply do not recognize angels in their midst or their guiding, saving ministrations no matter how often they come. Our minds quickly rationalize or intellectualize anything not immediately understandable.

When however, angels have averted danger or possible disaster to one close to them, one tends to acknowledge their beneficial presence with great gratitude, as happened in the following: One day after a tremendous snowstorm, Mark, who was then about eight or nine, offered to go shopping for me. I was ill, the cupboard was bare of essentials, the five children seemed too hungry to wait until their father returned from delivering a baby. The store wasn't far, but there was a big hill to climb coming home. Finally, I agreed and sent Mark off with a list, money, words of caution, and a prayer. When he returned, he was ashen and shaking. I apologized, thinking that the two bags, which were falling apart, had been too much for him to carry.

Mark told me that that was not it. He said something had happened, but he was afraid I would laugh and think he was crazy. When I reassured him, though still shaken, he began to share:

I was doing fine until I was about halfway up Huntville Road (the big hill). Then, I heard a voice say, "Look out, Mark." I kind of looked both ways, but I didn't see anyone or anything. The voice said again, this time louder, "Get out of the way, Mark." And, before I could even look, someone gave me a big shove way up into the snow bank. And just as I landed, a huge snow-remover truck came by scraping the street. The man never saw me! Mom, there was *no one* there. So, who shoved me? Who saved me?

Having had at least two similar experiences of being quite literally saved from disaster by just such an angel voice and nudge, I was ready to share with Mark and the other children that angels live in our midst. And, that whenever we hear such a clear, insistent voice—*listen and heed*—as long as the voice does not ask us to do something that would hurt another or be inappropriate, or would not be in your best interest, for that would not be an angel of Light.

Another more recent illustration of angel assistance was when my sister, Gail, and I were trying on our third visit to Fort Myers to help Dad understand that it was no longer safe or fair to Mom to be living alone so far from family; and he continued his resistance, refusing to talk about it. The time had come, however. So I implored the angels to help us. Finally, one morning at breakfast, I found myself asking Dad what he planned to do after lunch. "Just watching my usual bang-bangs on TV," he replied. When I told him I wanted a date with him after lunch, he began to shake and said, "I'll talk about anything except moving. We're not ready yet." I simply said quietly, "Dad, no one is going to make you move." And I left the table.

Gail and I took off to do some errands. On the way home, spontaneously, I pulled off the road and stopped, saying, "Gail, I'm not sure if you're aware that we all have angels with us. Now, Dad's guardian angel must be bored and asleep from so much inane TV." (Actually, our angels are ever present no matter how dull or frantic our lives may be, I'm sure.) "So let's just sit here and ask silently in prayer for our angels and Dad's angel to have an angelic conference to help us help Dad see the need to move." Gail agreed.

After a few minutes we left for home, ate lunch, and I told Dad we'd meet him in his den. I strongly "suggested" to Mom that she *had* to go rest in their bedroom, reminding her that on our last two visits when we had a short conversation about moving, Dad would always turn to her saying, "We're doing just fine, aren't we Merle," and Mom would demurely reply, "Yes, dear," even though she would cry over the phone on every call we had how she couldn't cope anymore. She didn't want to hurt Dad's feelings. Dad and Mom were both dealing with a lifetime buildup of fear.

As I started toward the door, I noticed Gail slipping out the front door to head for the pool. I stopped her and firmly asked, "Where are you going? You need to be there with Dad and me." She replied, "I just can't do it!" So I "compromised" by assuring her I just needed her to bring her angel to help out. She joined us.

Once settled in the den, Dad repeated the old refrain, "We're not ready to move." And I responded, "I hear you, Dad. But it's only fair, we need to know, what is it that's holding you here: the neighbors (about whom he regularly complained)? the church (which they no longer could attend)? the weatherman (who he enjoyed as a daily TV friend)? or what? We need you to help us understand. So let's just close our eyes and try to figure out what it is that's holding you back?" And I closed my eyes.

After several minutes, I peeked at Dad and saw a big tear rolling down his cheek. "What is it you'll miss, Dad?" I quietly asked. After a moment, Dad slapped his knee and in a determined, clear voice answered, "Not a damn thing! Go and get Mom. I want to tell her I think it's just about time for us to move closer to Gail in Las Vegas. And we need to get started before you girls leave."

Gail dashed into the bedroom and got Mom. When Dad told her the good news, she burst into tears, hugged him, told him she loved him, and cried, "I've been hoping and praying we could do that! Thank you so much!"

A book could be written about the three months we took from that day until they moved into the perfect apartment that Gail had found a few blocks from her house. Mom and Dad did not have one day of adjustment. Within a week Dad was saying, "I can't understand why we didn't do this sooner!"

And it was angels all the way! Gail and I estimate that over two dozen potential glitches, some major, were wondrously resolved—most, almost immediately—as we called on our angels. In fact, I've often kidded that Gail, who had never considered angels as having anything to do with our lives, was now out on the street corners of Las Vegas preaching about angels, she was so in touch with them. The truth is, her life has become greatly enhanced as she continues to call on their comforting, guiding presence.

How the angels ministered to Jesus, we do not know in detail. But the very fact that it was recorded in Scripture gives us reason to pause and reflect on how angels have ever been present to us. We can say with Shakespeare, "There are more things in heaven and earth, Horatio, than are dreamt of in your philosophy."

So as Jesus began to discern the mission he had come to fulfill, he confronted the spiritual dangers and possible pitfalls that might arise . . . the three prongs of the devil's pitchfork—money, fame, and power. These three dangerous and tempting prongs often seem to be considered values in our society today: the unequal, usually patriarchal, hierarchical structure within corporations, institutions, and, all too often, the churches; the power of the principalities of our day, of the press; the greed displayed by the media image-makers tempting us to want more and more of what we do not need, quite often seeming like an addictive poison; trespassing into the affairs of third-world countries, where we offer goods that promise, but that all too often only add to their plight all in the name of freedom, and usually with a hidden agenda not in their best interest; the yearning to be a star, to get to the top, to sit at the head table. Many individuals and beneficial groups are offering humane and sensitive programs. But they still seem the exception given the potential for the sharing of resources that are abundant in the world. All this is not so much a matter of right and wrong. Rather, one must question the *intent* of the heart? What is the highest good of LoveConsciousness? We do well to discern who is being served: the ego-self or Love?

By his choices, Jesus grew in strength and conviction. In silence, solitude, and prayer, he met temptation face-to-face. And, as a result of the testing, the will of the Most High revealed itself within him. Jesus took the momentum of tradition, affirmed it, and moved on. And with this quantum leap in consciousness, the future became an open book to be written. The role that Jesus denied in this last temptation prepared him for the time when the multitudes came and were about "to take him by force and make him king. He fled back to the hills to be alone" (John 6:15). Jesus chose to walk the narrow and lonely road that leads to abundant life, eternal life.

Jesus' forty days of wrestling with Lucifer concluded with a firm, unequivocal decision. By denying the temptations to gain the whole world of ego-illusory power and fame, he chose to embrace the Realm of Love, the soul's true home. Jesus chose to live so authentically, he shows us the Way, the Truth, and the Life that we, too, can *live*. This is not a one-time Consciousness; Jesus clearly encourages us to do all he did in Awakening to Love, One in Being with all . . . *in our own unique way*. We honor this great gift of Love as we chose to serve, co-creating together in the Plan for Earth.

To walk the wilderness road with Jesus is to recognize that each of us is LoveConsciousness in progress, a spark of the Universal Consciousness. To awaken in LoveConsciousness implies a process of integration, of accepting and walking through our fears and weaknesses, of releasing our prejudices, and recognizing the uselessness of our obsessions and passions. To come to know Reality is to find truth, truth that is unveiled within our Inner Being. And, inasmuch as we seek this truth, which often lays buried deep within us, the walls erected by the false ego-self will come tumbling down. We shall come to live into the Truth that sets us free; where fear can no longer find a home.

We are always being invited by LoveConsciousness to become the fullness of who we were born to be, to live and to share in the very life of Love within and with us. Each of us can find the road into and through the desert, where we plunge into our loneliness, our hunger, and our thirst. For here, we will be tempted; here we will be purified. And here we will hear the Voice of Wisdom (by whatever name) speaking to our hearts.

And, we can expect angels to come to minister to us.

As Jesus' time in the desert illustrates, one of the positive values of entering this time of testing is to engage in a sifting process in order to choose and accept our *highest* good. Often several options are possible, all of which are good. We are invited to choose all that is most life-giving in order to grow spiritually and mature in faith, to awaken in LoveConsciousness, and to actively serve in Love's Plan for Earth: home to us all. Thus, as we come out of the fears and darkness of the wilderness, we are freer to embrace the Love and Light that we are.

The Great Invocation has been prayed around the world in one form or another for decades. A most appropriate universal prayer for today's wounded world, to pray it aloud adds to its effectiveness:

> *From the point of Light within the Universal Mind*
> *Let Light stream forth into our human minds*
> *May Light renew the Earth.*
> *From the point of Love within the Universal Heart*
> *Let Love stream forth into our human hearts*
> *May Love return to Earth.*
> *From the Center of the Universal Will*
> *Let Purpose guide our little human wills*
> *The Purpose we are all called to serve.*
> *From the center which we call humanity*
> *Let the Plan of Love and Light work out*
> *And may it seal the door where fear and evil dwell.*
> *Let Light and Love and Power restore the Plan on Earth.*

5

The Road to Jericho

*A*wakening to our own unique Soul-journey, we begin to recognize that to follow the roads that Jesus walked seems natural, as if we've already been guided to our particular place on the path. And, by discovering how our capacity for love increases as we root out our fears and doubts, we are better prepared to meet our neighbor face-to-face. Like the lawyer in Scripture, we may ask, "What must I do to inherit eternal life?" Or, "What must I do to for soul-survival?" As Jesus so often did, he answered the lawyer's question with a question. "What is written in the Law? What is your reading of it?" The lawyer answered with another quotation from Scripture: "You must love the Lord your God with all your heart, with all your soul, with all your strength, and with all of your mind, and your neighbor as yourself." Satisfied with the answer, Jesus replied, "Do this and Life is yours" (Luke 10:25–28).

What do you suppose the lawyer's view of eternal life might have been? Possibly, an image many of us were taught as children: a perfect heavenly existence such as the Garden of Eden, before Adam and Eve ate fruit from the Forbidden Tree with little to do except enjoy the angels playing harps. At least that's what "they" tried to teach me. Yet, would that not be a regression, a kind of entropy, and boring. Jesus' answers usually imply much more than literal interpretation. We see by his actions that Jesus' life is an ongoing, active process of loving, which we, too, can live as our consciousness is awakened. To *do this* means to engage our lives lovingly and to act justly, with mercy and compassion, involved in soul-mending, soul-nurturing, soul-survival, for ourselves as well as neighbors and nations around the world, the environment, and the planet: our earth home. We are invited to grow and evolve into individuals with inner strength and an ever-expanding capacity to focus our intention on and through Love. In my experience, eternal life seems to be more of a dynamic way-of-being in *this* world rather than a state of static "happiness" forever after we die to this life. Eternal life is forever *now*, whether here on earth or when we are birthed into new Life beyond the veil. The very nature of Love is a gift beyond description. Yet, all we need do to enter into the fullness of this blessed life is to love God, ourselves, and our neighbors around the globe *as ourselves*. All? Who among us can? Yet, once we have experienced that LoveConsciousness embodies everything, when we fully *know* the Oneness of All, we will understand without question that Love *is* forever throughout the heavenly realms as well as here on earth.

We are invited to give all, to do all, in and through Love for our own well-being as well as for others. Jesus clearly demonstrated that love is a verb, not a noun. Love is a response, a reaching out toward others. St. John of the Cross discovered in his life that "Where there is no love, put love, and there you will find love." Love is not just the belief that "We love because God first loved us," true as that may be. Love is a total and authentic response that can be chosen and lived out. Yet, we must be freed from our fears in order to live fully in the present moment responding to life, to others, to God, with love. We need to be liberated to move into the flow of events, to be in harmony with ourselves and the universe. We must be in touch with our innermost Being to experience the timelessness and mystery of authentic living as a loving presence . . . one day—or moment—at a time. For *Now* is all we have. Time is irrelevant in the Realm of Love. Time as we experience it here on earth is linear, eternity is timeless; love in the material realm is time-oriented, *chronos*, and eternal spiritual love is experienced as *kairos*, timeless.

We are incapable of truly and freely loving God and/or our global neighbors until we have met ourselves in the inner depths, acknowledged our fears and walked through them until they no longer are troubling. For only as we are creatively in harmony with ourselves are we available to be authentically present to others. The world is seductive. We so often feel alienated and estranged from Divine Love, from our neighbors, from ourselves. Yet, our hearts are made for love . . . for Love. The potential and capacity of the heart for love is as immense as the ocean; all too often we are satisfied with just drops of love here and there—hardly enough for our close ties, never mind our neighbors. Some may feel that in loving others, they are taking love away from someone else, as if there is a limited quantity of love to go around. In reality, the more we are able to love authentically, the more love lives in our Being, radiating out to the world. There is no scarcity of Love; Love simply *is* boundless, infinite abundance. We tend to forget that our essence, our true Self, *is* Love. How many ways can I, do I, practice the presence of Love in action from my own loving heart? A provocative question to ponder.

And like the lawyer, we must discover who our neighbors are in today's world. Assuming the lawyer was a good Jew of the times, he would know that Yahweh had given Moses several definitions of neighbor. In the Hebrew Scripture, a neighbor was a member of one's own group. Loving one's friends is natural, fairly easy, and a universal understanding, whether acted upon or not. "You shall not set your heart on your neighbor's house, spouse or possession" (Exodus 20:17). And, "You will not exact vengeance on the members of your race, but will love your neighbor *as* yourself" (Leviticus 19:18). And then, Yahweh extends the definition of neighbor to include resident foreigners: "If you have resident aliens in your country, you will not molest them. You will treat them as though they were native born and love them *as* yourself" (Leviticus 19:33). So, in answering the lawyer, Jesus brings new meaning to the command of Yahweh. He *universalizes*

the concept of neighbor with the parable of the Samaritan, someone the Jews in that day regarded as *outside the pale* (John 4:9).

> A man was once on his way down from Jerusalem to Jericho and
> fell into the hands of bandits; they stripped him, beat him, and
> then made off, leaving him half dead. Now a priest happened to
> be traveling down the same road, but when he saw the man, he
> passed by on the other side. In the same way, a Levite who came
> to the place saw him and passed by on the other side. But a
> Samaritan traveler who came on him was moved with compassion
> when he saw him. He went up to him and bandaged his wounds,
> pouring oil and wine on them. He then lifted him onto his own
> mount and took him to an inn and looked after him. The next
> day, he took out two denarii and handed them to the innkeeper
> and said, "Look after him, and on my way back I will make good
> any extra expense you have." Which of these three he asked the
> lawyer [and asks us today] do you think proved himself a neigh-
> bor to the man who fell into the bandits' hands?" The lawyer
> replied, "the one who showed pity towards him." Jesus said to
> him, "Go, and do the same yourself" (Luke 10:29–37).

The journey from Jerusalem to Jericho is about seventeen
miles and falls more than 3,400 feet. A wilderness road, it was a
barren, desolate, and lonely road with many opportunities for
Bedouin robbers to ply their trade. As in all of the parables, Jesus
is describing an outer reality *and* the inner journey of the soul by
means of symbols, which reveal eternal truths to us.

The first person we meet is a wounded individual, who has
been beaten, stripped and left to die. What feelings well up in
you as you imagine the suffering of this individual? Do you know
anyone who has been so brutally abused? Places like this exist all
over the world today from the wilderness of urban parks and
playgrounds to our institutions, businesses, military and government, from all the horrors of war with its related refuge camps
and its myriad victims of violence visited upon so many of our
global neighbors, to the dens of kidnapped sexual slaves, even to
nursing homes and, all too often, our own home. We are never
immune from those who would rob us of our names, possessions,

our dignity, our right to grow, develop, and mature, as well as our very lives. We are a wounded society, a wounded and wounding world. Even our very Earth has been deeply ravaged and is *critically* wounded. This victim at the side of the road, and all victims, *are* us, you and me. What in us allows us to pass them by? We cannot afford to pass by on the other side! We do so at the peril of total chaos, police states, environmental catastrophe, and more.

Yet, we all miss the mark from time to time. I must confess that recently, I did just that. A man walking along the sidewalk using a walker called out to me. I couldn't hear him and I was hurrying to get home for what seemed an important reason. I called out that I couldn't hear him and that I was in a terrible hurry. I waved and "passed him by." Even before I reached my "important" goal, I felt extreme remorse, my heart pounded with the sense of having betrayed both the unknown man, my neighbor, and my own soul. The pain I experienced and how long I carried it, even to waking up in the night with tears, is a clear example of how, when we hurt or ignore another who *is* in a real spiritual sense ourselves, we do damage to our own soul. I prayed for forgiveness and intend never to do that again. And I trust a way will present itself for me to make amends and to respond with compassion and integrity, if not with the same man, another. It matters not who, for we are all One. Nothing is more important than responding to life, moment by moment, in a loving way. The good news is called forgiveness. We do not have to beat ourselves up or carry our poor choices around forever . . . for, guilt is of the ego, while forgiveness is always a mutual blessing.

To relate to the wounded one, we must look to ourselves, within our own psyches. Can you identify with this wounded individual? You may never have been physically violated, yet we all carry wounds, be they neglect, rejection, abandonment, misunderstandings, being treated unjustly, or oppressed. Perhaps, we have wounded or betrayed ourselves in some way—most often unconsciously. I discovered just this kind of inner wound through a troubling dream, which I share to illustrate the power and gift of our dreams, one way to work with them, and the love that ensues as we befriend the fears that rob us of creativity and expressing our true Self, the essence of our Inner Being: I went down the cellar stairs and was amazed to discover the basement (often symbolizing the unconscious depths in dreams) was large and totally swept clean. Lighted by a large, single bulb hanging down from the center of the ceiling, similar in appearance, in this life, to where my first deep wound occurred when I was five-years-old in the hospital with polio. I saw a door leading to a sub-basement. As I entered through it and started down the step, someone scurried into a closet to hide. I quickly noted what looked like pieces of furniture neatly covered with cloths to keep them clean. But, feeling very uncomfortable knowing that there was someone hiding in the closet, I went out, locked the door and returned upstairs to the house.

I had passed the person in the closet by. I tried to ignore the dream, but it haunted me for days. The locked door and whoever was behind it felt like a major issue in my life, though I knew not what; I just wanted it to disappear. Finally, after being nagged by the memory of the dream for two weeks, I chose to dialogue with the dream as a way of discovering what it might be asking of me, another way of facing my fear:

Me: Empty basement, you scare me. It is as if you are too clean. What does Scripture say? If you clean out one demon, watch out that seven more don't move in!

Basement: You have been cleaning me out for years. Now that the work is bearing fruit, you are distressed.

Me: I never thought to sweep you clean. This takes me by surprise. But what is in the adjoining room—who did I lock in the closet?

Basement: (Smiling at me) That is what surprised you; yet you were not really all that afraid. The closet holds the key.

Me: And the child in there? Assuming it was a child . . .

Basement: Yes, the Child is that creative energy which has become available to you. This is what you most fear.

Me: Can I unlock the door right now and let "her" out?

Basement: Take a moment and imagine yourself doing just that.

Me: It is quite dark in here, but I can see old piles of stuff waiting for me to go through. I feel afraid of being locked in the room. (I was once locked in the closet by a "friend" of the family when I was about three.) I go to the little closet door at the left wall. I open it and look in to total darkness. There are some skeleton bones to the left. I crawl in with a flashlight and find her huddled in a corner to the right. She is afraid of me! Now isn't that sad?

Basement: You haven't treated her very kindly in the past. You have become so serious and work-oriented, you have acted as if she did not exist. Why would you expect her to even recognize, much less, know you?

Me: Don't be afraid. I've come to be with you and to welcome you back into my life. (Silence.) She cowers further into the corner. . . . I sit and wonder how I can get through such *fear*. She is so afraid of me. Sitting in the center of the closet, I cry and cry and cry. . . . Finally, I speak to her again. Will you, can you, begin to forgive me? I remember you now. You were always with me when I was little. You had such beautiful energy, such warm ways, such hope, and charity. You led me on merry chases, you helped me to see and love the little things. Where did we part? When did I begin to ignore your harmonizing presence?

She: Do you really know me? It has been *so* long!

Me: Of course, I do remember you . . . and, I . . . I love you. Oh, I so regret that I treated you so shabbily, not even as an orphan. I treated you the way that I felt at my depths . . . as a nothing, as if you did not exist. I am so sorry.

She: (coming a bit closer) I've never fully developed or matured. I am still so tiny and fragile. I am still so afraid of you—that you will expect more of me than I am ready to give.

Me: Are you willing to be a part of me once more? Could you love me, trust me, lead me on a merry chase, perhaps? I had forgotten how much we need one another.

She: Oh, I want to—more than anything—but slowly, at first. I feel like sleeping Beauty who as just been awakened. I will be slow and perhaps unsteady for a time. But already, I can feel my energy pulsating. Oh, I am so happy to be back with you—Nancy, who has become Nan. I like that.

Me: I am glad and grateful. Lead me as you are ready. Have I forgotten your name? What shall I call you?

She: I am "the one who laughs," so you can call me "Laughing Star" . . . although "Dancing Star" seems more a part of you. Perhaps you can simply call me "Star." You have found the star that you have been searching for—found and lost—over and over.

And the closet filled with a radiant light. I took Star by the hand and we came out into the sub-basement. It, too, began to radiate light, beaming into the clean basement that now dazzled in the light of Star's brilliant glow. I thanked the basement and thought to myself, "Now, all is well."

This healing dialogue filled me with wonderment, a gentle joy, and a blessed inner peace. Outwardly, I began to act more spontaneously and creatively. Yet, it would take years of re-building trust with "Star" to be free enough to enjoy "a merry chase" – i.e., to do something just for the fun and joy of it. This has been far more difficult than I ever would have believed!

After a decade or so, at an autumn festival in Hannibal, Missouri, I was totally relaxed as I watched a group of "cloggers" dancing. When they called people up to do the "chicken dance," spontaneously, I jumped up and took the hands of a child on each side of me. I had never deigned to get up at weddings to dance the chicken dance, which others seemed to find delightful, including my more fun-loving sister. Suddenly, I realized I was the only adult in the circle; this dance was for the children. The "adult me" was about to flee, when Dancing Star took over and I discovered the Dance dancing me! It was *so* freeing! I could get used to this: the zen of dancing!

How many among us have had our inner child wounded? Experience has shown that we must become like little children to enter fully the Dance of Life, so we can be healed. Our wounds live within us waiting—ever waiting—for us to call them forth as Jesus called Lazarus forth from the tomb to new life. The more we are willing to bring our wounds into the light of Christ's Healing Love, the more we will be a healing presence to those who suffer, who are lonely and vulnerable, to the victims of racism, third-world oppression, to nations robbing and warring with other nations, to big corporations, who greedily, and seemingly blindly, rape and exploit Mother Earth, all too often rationalizing and distorting well-documented scientific reports of our fragile planetary home. LoveConsciousness *is* the solution. May we choose to join the growing numbers of life-giving communities who act in the name of Love to heal the terrible plight of all Creation? One by one *we can do this.*

Next, we meet the priest and the Levite, who choose to pass by the wounded one. What does it mean that two good and upright citizens would ignore someone in such distress? These two individuals had "important" roles being the carriers of tradition and protectors of the rules and laws. They were cautious for, indeed, it was dangerous territory in which they were traveling. The robbers might still be close by. And, no doubt, they had very busy schedules. They "did good" whenever it was convenient and appropriate to their role; they were efficient in their organizations and comfortable in the hierarchical structures. To get involved might cost them far too much in terms of time, energy, reputation, and money, not to mention the fear of contamination should any blood come upon them. And, it is here, that I plead guilty to my recent "fall from grace." To walk quickly by seemed the most expedient and sensible thing to do in that moment. Someone else walking along, who might have more leisure would surely attend the needs of this man. Yet, forgiveness cleanses the slate. No matter what our "sin," we are born to love, not to wallow in guilt.

Alas, how much of the priest and Levite live in us. To recognize bits and pieces of oneself in them is humbling and, if consciously honored, will lead to an aspiration and intention to be ever more mindful in the present moment, to re-examine one's priorities, and, paradoxically, to grow in compassion. Our pride, ambition, and vanity so often get in the way of doing what our deepest and best would call us to do. Like Paul, we can say, "I do not understand my own behavior. I do not act as I mean to, but I do the things that I would rather not do" (Romans 7:15).

Unless we recognize our own insensitivity, learn to say "no" to ego-illusions that separate us from loving choices, make amends in some way, ask forgiveness, and let go of our poor choices, we become more wounded with the aftermath of shame, guilt, and doubt our core essence of Love. The priest and Levite in us act subtly; they are often difficult to see. Being the parts of ourselves that do good works, they can seduce us into feelings of self-righteousness and blind us to the truth. The greatest value of truth is, as has been noted, that it sets us free, liberates us, to become what we already are in the depths.

The priest-Levite has come to light for me in many guises giving me many opportunities to face them, learn from them, and hopefully, to allow their energy to be transformed into Love. Many years ago, I discovered a sub-personality who lived within. Participating in a group exercise, we were encouraged to get in touch with a fragment of our personality, a sub-personality. We were led in meditation to a path and invited to explore it until we came to a door. We were to knock on the door to see who lived there. In this particular exercise the pathway led to the top of a mountain covered with clouds. When I felt a "structure," which I took to be a door, I knocked. After a few seconds, the head of a huge giraffe came down out of the clouds. When I asked her name, she, with her nose in the air, deigned to tell me her name was Ms. Aloof and that she preferred not to be bothered by the things of this world. Talk about being surprised. I could not believe any part of my personality was aloof! I took the road of denial. Then a numinous dream followed soon after, which supported what I was avoiding and did not care to see:

I was climbing a high mountain with amazing ease and felt exhilarated as I neared the top. Then, I saw other mountains in the distance and imagined myself leaping easily from peak to peak. Yet, when I reached the top, my heart seemed to stop. A Christ figure stood there before me with arms outstretched looking me straight in the eyes with great Love and Compassion. I wanted to weep. Pointing to the valley below where there were houses, businesses, and people, he said simply, "Feed my sheep."

Just that, and my life turned in a new direction, which led me to work in a mental-health facility as well as at the nearby state prison for women—a humbling and most appropriate response to living on mountain tops with my head in the clouds. Spiritual inflation could have distracted me and kept me from my true path.

And then a Samaritan comes along, one whose people were hated by the Jews more out of racism than religious differences. The Samaritan, being wounded within, has known suffering and rejection. Having no roles to protect, no defensive fears, no haste to be somewhere, is free. And the suffering of the wounded person immediately touched his own heart. Compassion moved him to action. And what did he do? This despised Samaritan is extravagantly lavish. He uses his oil and wine for healing, gives his mount up to the suffering one and walks to the nearest inn, which may have been miles away. There, he not only cares for this individual, he gives the innkeeper two denarii, which would be several days pay and promised more, if needed.

The Samaritan dared to risk—and more. He gave all he had—and more. We are invited as we walk this road to do the same —and more. We are invited to healing, wholeness, and holiness—and more. We are invited to share all we are with our neighbors, whoever, wherever they may live with and as LoveConsciousness in action. We do not know who the wounded one is, but it could very well have been a Jew, who would have been feared as an enemy to the Samaritan. How do you suppose the wounded one felt when he regained consciousness and was told all that the Samaritan had done for him? How do you think he might have responded? Can you imagine anyone loving you this extravagantly? The Beloved does! What was once said of Mother Teresa, could well be said of the Samaritan: "Because she/he was free to be nothing, God could use her/him for anything."

Have you ever been tempted to be that lavish in your love? Are you aware of the Samaritan who lives in your inner being? What is you compassion quotient? Compassion comes from the Greek meaning *guts*—such strong feelings arising from deep within a person for another that it implies his stomach turned over, it made him ill to see this suffering.

Who comes to mind as compassionate in today's world? We think of Mother Teresa's life, of those who stand by the oppressed, those we read of who have done some heroic deed through Love, the outpouring response to the 9/11 attack or the more recent Tsunami and Katrina disasters. Compassion dwells at the deepest core within each one of us. Sometimes it is well hidden; yet, often it is not recognized because it seems so natural—within families, friendships, and with those who answer the cries of the poor. To have compassion for our neighbors means to feel in ourselves what they are feeling; to deal with their feelings, their plight, as if they were our own; to make them our own through some act of kindness, prayer, presence. In truth, our neighbors are ourselves: for what we do for others, we do for LoveConsciousness. We are interconnected to *all* of Creation, so totally interwoven that as the Earth, other nations, and all people are—so, too, are we, aware or unaware.

To ponder that we carry the scars of earth's body within our very souls, the wounds and deaths of the victims and even the perpetrators of violence, war, slavery, is to recognize how complicit we can be in "passing by on the other side." Discernment is crucial here. To feel guilty, blame or attack others, become apathetic or fearful only adds to the myriad concerns that we face.

Throughout Jesus' life and ministry in all that he said and did, we are given the greatest gift the world has ever known: the key to Love. By deed, Jesus exemplified the way to Love: defenselessness. This is a surprising route that encompasses facing the very core fears and "values" that ego-illusion would have us live by. To love the Source of our being with our whole heart, mind, and soul is a call to surrender *everything* we are and hold dear onto

Love's Will, not our will be done. This total abandonment may seem to leave us completely vulnerable to all our ego-fears, on the one hand, or to be like puppets being orchestrated from on high with no choice of our own, on the other hand. Yet, simply put, ultimately, the choice is always ours: the way of love and truth . . . or, the way of fear and illusion. The good news is that we are not left to walk either road alone.

The way of Jesus' defenselessness is most vividly lived during the three days leading up to Easter. During the feast of Passover, Jesus displayed his total humility and surprised everyone present as he tied a towel around his waist, took a basin of water and began one by one to wash the disciple's feet. Then, he asked those present if they understood that as a teacher, he was giving them a model to follow. So, one lesson all along our journey into Love is humility, a defenseless action that portended Jesus' night in the Garden, his silence when confronted by the authorities, his compassion for the beggar on the cross, as well as those who nailed him to the cross, all in surrender to God's Will. Jesus drank the bitter cup of utter humility and the world has never been the same.

With humility, we will learn the lesson of serving others all along our journey into Love. The hidden gift—and there are many hidden gifts on these roads—is that in serving and loving others *as* ourselves, we become beneficiaries of all we offer to others. We discover that our Oneness with all has a ripple effect that extends outward to the world. Everything that we do, all that we think, makes a difference to our soul and to the Soul of the world for blessing or for increasing the fear-quotient that depends on attack for its "security." The road to Love is a humble road. In defenselessness is our strength.

My greatest experience of compassion for another and defenselessness seems to be quite different from what we normally call love—perhaps, only in intensity of feeling. Ironically, this was when I was being robbed at gunpoint. My response was so unlikely, I can only believe LoveConsciousness was very much in charge. I share it with you at the risk of being thought naïve.

Coming home from grocery shopping late one night while living in Detroit, Sister Susan and I were just turning into the blind alley that led to the back door when a young man with a hood over his head approached us from out of the bushes. Susan immediately began what soon became a mantra. Quietly behind me, she invoked, *Dear Lord, have mercy.* I gave him a friendly greeting. He ignored me and pulled out a gun demanding all our money. I couldn't believe the mixture of love and sadness that welled up in me. "I have all the money," I said, "but I don't believe in robbery; so, if you need the money, I'll give it to you," and I did. He wasn't at all polite about it, and grabbed my wallet. I told him that I was giving him all the money, but *not* my papers and I took it back from him (after he had discovered the hidden, backup twenty dollar bill that I had forgotten about). Meanwhile, Susan's mantra continued, *Dear Lord, have mercy.*" Then, much to my surprise, he stepped back, apologized, asked for forgiveness, and said he really did need the money. Again he spoke, "I hope you won't hold this against my people." I told him that of course I wouldn't. I was *giving* him the money, but I really hoped it wouldn't be used for drugs or alcohol. I wished him a good evening and blew him a kiss as he scaled the fence he'd evidently climbed to get in the "secured" property. And, even then, Sister Susan continued the mantra, *Dear Lord, have mercy*, which may have saved our lives. Who knows?

Years later, I realized something about that encounter was nagging at me. I took an hour or so for meditation and reflection, and realized that I had tainted the "gift" by telling him how not to spend it. How easy it is for our egos to try to seize control of others. I continue to wing him a prayer when he comes to mind. Sometimes, we do not know the depth of our own capacity to care. We are surprised by the love in us. I suspect, that having faced my fears over the years and having encountered the robber and wounded parts of myself, I intuitively recognized the inner woundedness of this outer robber and felt compassion rather than anger and fear. So, as I often work out inner discontent by writing a poem, one day the following freed me from any lingering negativity from what turned out to be a life-giving encounter.

For, it was through this event that I fully realized that fear no longer enslaved me. What a grace!

> The hooded hood slipped out of the bushes
> With pointed gun demanding
> "all of your money."
> "Dear Lord, have mercy," prayed
> Sister Susan behind me.
> "I have all the money, but
> I don't believe in robbery" –
> Could I really have said that?
>
> "Dear Lord have mercy."
> "I'll give you all the money –
> even that squirreled away
> for a rainy day."
> And I did.
> "Dear Lord, have mercy."
> "Thank you," he said, "I really need this.
> Can you forgive me and not
> hold it against my race?"
> "Dear Lord, have mercy."
>
> "Ah, but this is a gift –
> may you use it wisely
> and not for drugs.
> No need to forgive."
> "Dear Lord, have mercy."
> I waved and blew him a kiss
> as he scaled the fence from
> whence he had come.
> "Dear Lord, thank You."
>
> Grateful for life, yet disquieted within,
> I went to my room to pray.
> "Dear Lord, have mercy."
> Oh, how difficult to give freely!
> What presumption to tell him
> how to use the gift!
> "Dear Lord, have mercy."
> Is it not I in need of forgiveness?

For fear sees a hooded hood;
compassion sees a human being;
fear presumes the worst,
compassion assumes wholeness.
"Dear Lord, have mercy."
And thus my soul did garner
a new gift of growth.
Ah, the Mystery of our interconnectedness
with All where all
is gift!
And You, O Merciful Heart, are
the Inexhaustible Gift!
Love at the heart of Life

The robber acts violently within us against the integrity of our wholeness, our holiness. We rob our bodies when we over-indulge, whether it be food, sex, alcohol, drugs, work that leads to stress, or with couch "potatoitis." We know our sensibilities have been robbed when we are filled with fear, depression, anger, anxiety, guilt, frustration, jealousy, when we are doubting of ourselves. We rob our minds by trivia, excessive outside stimuli, apathy, ennui, media mania, letting others think for us. And, saddest of all, our Inner Being, our very soul-life, is robbed when we worship the false gods of materialism so prevalent in the world and when we fail to develop into the fullness of our birth potential. It was Walt Kelly's Pogo who said, "We have met the enemy and he is us." Matthew put it this way, "A person's enemies will be of their own household." When fear rules our lives, how can we extend our love? Fear separates us from love; in love and with Love we are at One with all. Our very life and the life of the planet depends upon us waking up and staying awake if future generations are to have any quality of life! Otherwise, who will respond to the cries of millions of people who are hungry, homeless, and who yearn for peace, education, uncontaminated water, and health care?

LoveConsciousness invites us to a complete inner transformation. For without this, how can we possibly learn to identify with our sisters and brothers? We come to love our neighbor as we love ourselves when we face and forgive our false ego illusions—a letting go that we take great pains to resist. Our ego attachments are strong. They fight every inch of the way as we aspire to abandon ourselves into the hands of Love, as we loosen the chains of fear that keep us from discovering our true selves. Inasmuch as we allow Love's Spirit to work within us for deep inner transformation, we will be able to love our neighbors and *with them* help to build the realm of Love on Earth. Competition must give way to co-creation, to cooperation.

Until we can see how we lose ourselves to the world's wiles, how we betray ourselves unaware, it is difficult, if not impossible, to abandon ourselves in Service to the Beloved, or to others, without coloring all we offer with the paralyzing fears that lurk in our false self. This is not meant to sound too demanding; of course, we are all works in progress. If I speak in imperatives, I am simply amplifying the immediacy of our planet's present plight. As we become more conscious of our wounded, robber, role-directed aspects and develop attitudes of acceptance, compassion, and forgiveness, we move toward healing; we become more in touch with Samaritan-compassion within us; and, we join with others serving with LoveConsciousness, where with peace and true joy, we celebrate the Dance of Life.

When we accept Jesus' invitation to walk the roads he traveled with a conscious and often courageous commitment, the easier it becomes for our wounds to be assimilated and transformed; the more energy we will have for creativity, love, abiding peace, and joy. Growing more mature, more responsive to Love's nudges, and freer to be beneficial presences in the world, we will take joy in co-operating and co-creating with our neighbors around the globe. We will live more authentically in the Eternal Now, which is Life. We will express the Light we are in the world and radiate more brightly. We will shine.

The long road ahead may seem daunting. Yet as we *unite* to upbuild the world with LoveConsciousness, as we delight in diversity, as we learn from the rich tapestry of different cultures and religions, as we agree to disagree when solutions seem to elude us, as we recognize and reverence the interconnectedness and Oneness of all Creation, the momentum for healing our wounded world will grow into a universal Dance. Each of us can make a difference through forgiveness and choices that are in the highest interest of our Earth community. How we respond to those who are physically, mentally, or financially challenged, to the oppressed, to those in prison, in nursing homes, to all those who are wounded and in need, directly reflects on who we are individually, communally, and dictates our nation's credibility among other nations. The humble Samaritan qualities which reflect Jesus' teachings will all be needed as we take the journey on the road to Jerusalem.

6

❦

The Road to Jerusalem

The road to Jerusalem is a road most of us would prefer to avoid. It is the road to the cross. In our society, where easy living, comfort, eternal youth, wealth, competition are advertised and are highly valued, the cross can only be seen as dismal failure. We ignore it as long as we are able. Yet, if we choose to allow Jesus' way, truth, and life to instruct us, we are bound to meet the cross: the place where we die to all the false ego-illusions that are not the home of Love, not in our best interest. Our crosses can be catalysts to surrender to the One who has walked before us and who continues to journey with us every step of the way. It is the gateway to new life, peace, and joy.

This journey to Jerusalem that the disciples and Jesus began together is where Jesus most decisively demonstrates how consistently and authentically he lived the truth that sets us free, the truth of Who he is and Who we are called to be. It was in Jerusalem that Jesus totally surrendered to LoveConsciousness by being true to his mission, a model for all who would live with faith, authenticity, and integrity. To walk the road to Jerusalem means symbolically to travel from what seems to be a comparatively safe place, which costs little, to a place of risk, discomfort, and possible danger, that many might like to bypass; it could cost everything. Yet, to recognize the world's values as the illusions that they engender is to move toward a life of Love: our true Home and Being. To walk the road to Jerusalem tests the reality of our profession of faith. The disciples were not yet ready to see this truth. Like most of us, they kept missing the point.

We can count on meeting many of the same obstacles that the disciples met on the road to Jerusalem. James and John, the sons of Zebedee, in all naiveté and sincerity requested to sit on either side of Jesus in the unseen realm of Love. Along with their mother, they doubted and questioned the future. How discouraged Jesus may have felt to have come so far with the disciples and to have them understand so little. This same bid for special attention, to promote oneself, to be number one, is still rampant in our competitive way of life—individually, collectively, institutionally, politically, socially, economically. Competition so easily leads to jealousy, envy, injustice, illusion, greed, corruption in myriad disguises. Most often, competition is a kind of attack that leads to winners and losers. Cooperation and defenselessness, on the other hand, create communion, and community, which, if authentic and loving, blesses everyone with a sense of co-creating with the Beloved. When did Jesus ever compete?

Like James and John, I met one of my demons on the road to Jerusalem—that terrible demon of jealousy, an ego-desire to be special. For much of my life I had known the wretched feeling that jealousy brings, but had always been reluctant to call it by name. At a time when I was living in community, that demon was making my life so miserable that I had to stop and face jealousy head on. Recalling Walter Wink's injunction to name our demons in his trilogy on the Powers and Principalities,[14] I made a commitment to face that long-avoided fear head on.

One evening, an occasion arose of being taken over by jealousy as the community left to attend yet another celebration that didn't include me, though I couldn't understand why. I was left alone, putting away the dinner I had prepared. No one had remembered to inform me of other plans. When everyone left, I fled to my room and locked the door. ("Go into your closet to pray," I took quite literally that particular evening.) I informed the Powers that be that I would remain there until I had dealt with this ugly way-of-being that took so much of my energy. If I wasn't healed, I didn't see how I could remain in community, though I loved being there with others, living in urban Detroit, and working with the parish team and family.

Intuitively, I pulled my rocking chair to the center of the room and faced a watercolor that I had painted of a Christ head bearing the crown of thorns on another evening when I had been left alone to attend the door and phone. With a Vivaldi tape quieting playing "*Gloria*" in the background, I just sat staring at the painting, forcing myself to stay with the feelings of jealousy.

Over and over I asked myself if I wanted to spend the rest of my life enduring this unhealthy emotional pain that was a not-so-subtle way of attacking myself and the situation—fear and guilt in action. I analyzed what it was doing to my body: rapid pulse, clenched teeth, a touch of nausea, tense body, throbbing head. That *was* my prayer, the only prayer I could offer in the moment. Then, slowly, I relaxed.

After over two hours of remaining immersed in the painting, offering only a silent Cry, I was startled to hear what I've come to trust as the Voice of Love: "You have always known me as the Christ of Sorrows. Soon you will know me as the Christ of Joy. You are now being healed of your jealousy. Know also that someone else in the city that you may never know will be healed tonight as well." That's how love and healing work. We are not healed alone. We are all healed together. A great sense of peace and love washed over me, and the tears that came were not tears of anger, fear, illusion, guilt, or jealousy, but healing tears of great gratitude.

I believe we are that interconnected. As we are ready to walk this road, to name and face our fear demons and to surrender ourselves to Love, we take unknown others with us both here on earth and in the unseen Realm of Love. And just as James and John were surely forgiven by Jesus in his care-filled response to them, so we, too, are forgiven as we cry out to the Holy Counselor for help on the way to Jerusalem. That was over twenty years ago. Though I must admit to a twinge or two of the old demon, I can now smile and say inwardly, "Be gone, you old demon. I am healed!" And I am. As the Christ of Joy becomes more and more a presence in my life, I gratefully rejoice as others have done over the ages, I rejoice in Love's Companioning Presence always! Gratitude has become my soul's song of Love.

Time and time again on the road, Jesus instructs us, as he taught James and John and all the disciples, that worldly success does not make for greatness. Rather, our invitation is to just the opposite stance. The most authentic way-of-being is to be a servant to all as Jesus modeled with such fidelity in his mission and purpose of service. We are called to a voluntary humility that comes out of the processes of our baptism, naming, our wilderness experiences, how we treat all others, as well as our times in solitude, silence, and prayer, until our faithfulness to the Journey leads us to know LoveConsciousness so intimately that we become beneficial presences radiating peace, light, and love into the Soul of the world. Each of us has the capacity to walk our own way to Jerusalem, to suffer and endure our own crosses, trusting—ever trusting—that we will not be given more than we can bear, that strength and guidance will be provided. Then, as Jesus intended, we shall grow toward being the fullest human consciousness, the most authentic divine being that we are capable of becoming in this life. We will live more and more in the Heart of Love welcoming our sisters and brothers from everywhere home to the Oneness we are with the Source of our being.

Inasmuch as we do not consciously follow these universal roads that any individual or religion might embrace, we do ourselves a disservice; we are apt to become robots unaware. I most definitely do not mean to say or imply that this is the only road to follow. While Jesus' life is the paradigm for the Christian myth, the journey into love, peace, and wholeness shares much in common with other religious myths. Myth, here, simply means an archetypal Story that is a reality living in our collective psyches whether we are aware of it or not.

Judas[15] *seemed* not to see or envision Jesus' mission. His eyes remained focused on the earthly realm. Perhaps with the best of intentions, with a secret agenda of hastening the realm of Love on earth, Judas may have wanted only to force Jesus' hand to take on the reign of power then and there, perhaps, a prelude to the seemingly insatiable desire for instant gratification so rampant today. In doing so, however, Judas with a kiss of death boldly seemed to betray the One who trusted and loved him. When he realized the enormity of his betrayal, he could not bear the guilt and agony that his actions must have wrought. His own inner blindness must have kept him from knowing that Jesus' love would never end—no matter what. From Judas we learn what it means to betray. We all have an inner Judas, a place of darkness that we hold to ourselves. This is the place where we insist that our own will be done—in our way, in our time.

The disciples often failed miserably on this road to Jerusalem, just as we continue to fall from grace again and again. For, this road includes loneliness, doubts, rejection, suffering. Jesus knew this only too well. Death on a cross was the most shameful death possible at that time—reserved for the most heinous of criminals. To be so accused had to have been the lowest point of humilia-tion in Jesus' pilgrimage here on earth. Jesus must have felt it even more keenly because of his great love for family, friends, followers, and even those who falsely accused him. Yet, Jesus with full LoveConsciousness, offers this immense gift to the world, pointing to the way we, too, (without dying physically on the cross) can die to ourselves, our false self, and surrender our lives and souls into Love's sacred hands and heart. A Sufi prayer suc-cinctly puts a part of our journey on the road to Jeruselem in perspective:

> *I do not ask to see.*
> *I do not ask to know.*
> *I ask only to be used to do Thy Work*

—even to dying on our own crosses that can lead us to a life of service.

Knowing the inner thoughts of the disciples, their responses on the Jerusalem road must have been quite predictable to Jesus. Naming the impending betrayals of Judas and Peter, in some mysterious and total way, they were forgiven even before their acts were completed. In truth, their betrayal and denial seem to have been more keenly experienced in their own hearts. We assume that Judas, condemned by his own hand, recognized the terrible loss this would engender, could never forgive himself and felt that nothing remained to live for. Peter, having pretended ignorance once and simply denied twice that he had ever known Jesus, lived with the terrible guilt—the outer fear or ego manifestation of inner darkness—that followed betrayal until Love's Spirit erupted within him. I believe that Judas, too, knew the Light and felt Jesus' all embracing Love and forgiveness. Guilt, which may be a subtle way of boasting, will always deaden the Spirit without forgiveness.

Guilt, like carrying a heavy burden, weighs us down and clouds the soul. When family, friends, neighbors, or others clash with harsh words or attacks, it easily leads to alienation: energy-draining, physically depleting, toxic assaults on the psyche. When nations attack one another, the world Soul, the world's consciousness is affected in ways that impact our lives more than we can begin to understand! When forgiveness and reconciliation are neglected, guilt, pride, obsessive reenactments of the situation only exacerbate the problem. Whenever we attack another for any reason, we are, in essence, attacking ourselves to the same degree albeit in a different form. Hate begets hate—a harsh derivative of fear.

I love this simple, illustrative story I was told many years ago:

When two monks who had been traveling for some time came to a river that had to be crossed, a lovely woman stood at the bank in obvious distress. One monk asked if they could be of service. She told them that she had to get to the other side if she was to get home before dark. Being compassionate, he picked her up in his strong arms and easily crossed the river. He then put her down onto the shore and wished her a safe journey.

In stony silence, the second monk uttered not a word. Tension grew until they neared the monastery. Finally, the incensed monk, who felt pure and unsullied, stopped abruptly. "Brother," he exclaimed, "I feel I must reprimand you. Having broken your vow of chastity, you are in immediate need of confession and forgiveness. What possessed you to sweep that woman off her feet and hold her close to you all the way across the river?"

Pondering for a moment, the first monk quietly asked, "Oh, my dear brother, did you not see that I let her go when I put her ashore? Why are you still carrying her? Lessen your burden and let her go." Now, having both released her, the monks continued peacefully along the pathway home.

Like the monks we always have a choice. We can free ourselves from the heavy burdens of fear-driven emotions that all too quickly can become illusionary mind-games, obsessive tapes, blaming others. Forgiveness and understanding can set us on the road Home: living in the peace of LoveConsciousness. We can call on our guides and angels for help; we can call upon the Holy Spirit, Who knows the Way.

Jesus paved the way for all to follow by taking the narrow roads to life. With enemies all around him, hated by his own people, left to face the unknown alone by his sleeping disciples, Jesus faced temptation once again. In the desert he had denied the expectations of the times in order to follow the creative road that led to spiritual evolution and life in abundance. So, too, on the road that led to the Cross, Jesus continued to follow the way he had modeled so responsibly and authentically, trusting Abba even in the great Silence.

One of the ways that we learn the agony we cause when we betray another is through experiences of having been betrayed. Until then, it can be pretty much theory. Can you be in touch with a time when you have felt betrayed, or when you may have betrayed another? Are you aware of having betrayed yourself at any time? How does your body respond? Your feelings and thoughts? Your spirit? Have you forgiven those who have betrayed you? Or, have you asked forgiveness from those you may have betrayed—even of yourself? The betrayals that we undergo may seem minute compared to those of Jesus; still, they serve to awaken our consciousness, to help us walk through the ego-guilt and fear illusions that betrayal engenders, and to humble us through forgiveness, so that we might grow and mature into more authentic, responsible, and loving individuals. By way of illustration, the following are threads of betrayal that followed me, plagued me, and caused me to betray myself for much of my life—until I reconnected to Dancing Star, my Inner Child, my creative energy, in the "basement dream" shared earlier (p.93–96).

As early as my eighth birthday, I knew that I loved to write. When I received a five-year diary with a lock and key on my tenth Christmas, I was thrilled. I wrote with great joy and abandon for the first few months, *until* Dad, who was a traveling salesman, upon returning home from a long trip, asked to read my diary. I gasped! All the secrets of my young heart had been poured out and were meant for me alone. What I did not realize was that, with the best of intentions, I had been given the diary as a way of sharing my life with Dad so that he would not feel so cheated by his long absences. At ten years old, however, I only felt betrayed. My inner life had been invaded. And so, the diary became a pack of lies. I bragged of my goodness during his absences, maligned my poor sister, and wrote what I hoped would please him. Writing became a chore and a way of manipulation. I felt betrayed, so I betrayed in return.

In eighth grade, an English teacher gave us a creative homework assignment—a welcome relief from learning parts of speech. We were to write a poem all by ourselves. Excited, I tried for hours to write a poem, but nothing seemed good enough. Just before going to bed, a poem, "Nature's Garden," seemed to write itself. I *knew* it was good and showed it to my parents. They also liked it and Dad suggested that I change one word . . . from "stop" to "pause." His word seemed *so* right to me that I used it. Since I've expanded the poem over the years, I share only the five verses I wrote then:

> *Who made the flowers*
> *With colors so bright*
> *That give up their honey*
> *When bees pause in flight?*
>
> *Who made the birds*
> *That sing every day,*

Filling the air
With music so gay?

Who made the rain,
The sleet and the snow,
Giving earth water
That helps plants to grow?

Who made the sun
So round and so bright
That gives way to the moon
At the start of each night?

No man could perform
Such a wonderful task.
God made them all,
From the first to the last.

Two days later, the teacher announced that she had enjoyed the poems so much, she would read them to the class—in order, from worst to the best. My heart was racing when she got to the last one, assuming it was mine and the best. But, no, she never read my poem. After she finished the last poem, she gave me a piercing look and asked if I had anything to say. I allowed that I had turned in a poem, but she had not read it.

"Well, Miss Crerie," she said, "we are going to learn a new word today: *plagiarism*. You copied this poem out of a book, which is just like stealing. You could never write a poem this good, so you will stay after school every day until you show me the book you copied it from." I wanted to tell her I could prove that I wrote it because of the word my father changed, but I was afraid of that being called cheating. I felt trapped. Writing began to seem dangerous. I began to doubt a budding gift.

In tenth grade, the yearbook staff sponsored a writing contest. Our English teacher suggested we all write a story as a homework assignment. I wrote an autobiographical piece on what it felt like to be a wallflower, a social misfit. Having no idea that my story had been submitted, I was shocked and appalled when it won the prize and was published for all to read in the school "Spotlight." Now, I had announced publicly what I could hardly even admit inwardly—I was a failure, a social flop. I imagine the teacher meant well and thought I would be pleased to have my writing acknowledged; but all I felt was humiliation and, worst of all, I felt that I had betrayed myself. I missed noticing the blessing of being affirmed in what I most loved to do.

Thus, the joy of writing that I experienced early in my life became blocked by these and still other traumatic writing events. Because something compelled me to write, I kept journals, I edited or ghosted many books for friends. But my own writings I kept hidden away in boxes. Betrayal kills our creativity, paralyzes our creative Muse. The gifts that want to come to flower remain seeds, shadowed and hidden by weeds and rocky soil. A very small cross compared to Jesus' Cross, yet a part of my own Jerusalem journey.

Everyone's cross is unique. Some seem to be terrible crosses of physical pain and abuse, of terrible loss, of unspeakable agonies. Others are obstacles of mind, psyche, spirit that deaden the life we are given to share. If we do not seem to suffer a personal cross, we have only to turn on the news and we can pray with Jesus over Jerusalem and Palestine, over so many African countries, Iraq and all the surrounding countries, the worlds of drugs, oppression, sexual slavery, war, corruption, disease, famine, the planet's ongoing desecration. Our sisters and brothers around the world wait in hope for those who can help to carry their cross for a time, as Simon and Veronica helped Jesus on the way to Golgotha. We do not have to travel far to discover someone falling under the weight of their particular cross—individually, communally, or even as a nation. Nursing homes, prisons, mental institutions, hospices, hospitals, refugees. shut-ins at home—our world is sorely in need of more Simons and Veronicas to ease their burden on this road.

Keeping a journal on the Journey helps to ground the experiences we have—our joys, our sorrows, our growth as well as the times we miss the mark, the itinerary that we follow day by day.

I share an entry from my journal in 1985 while on retreat in Canada with the parish team:

> The day of Silence evoked an army of disharmonies. The evening of "Amerika" on television brought tears of dismay, disgust, and feelings of our seeming powerlessness. Today's Scripture on the yeast of the scribes and Pharisees seems timely! We are fed the bread of the advertisers, politicians, media. Are greed, propaganda, and pap to be the bread of our lives? I can understand the biblical way of expressing sorrow and grief—beating one's breast, rending one's clothes. I throw myself on the bed and weep, but somehow, it is a pale understatement of the Cry, which seems like Christ, within me. You, Who created us, help us to save ourselves from ourselves!
>
> I wish I could pray, but no words come. It is a matter of pure willpower to pray the Prayer of Abandonment. Yet, more than ever, I feel that each moment, each movement, *is* the prayer. I sense those whom I carry in my heart more keenly without words. In Christ-Love and in Christ-Love in them, I am changed—rather painfully today. Even so, each death in me that I grieve opens the door to new life. So, the tension of the opposites continues. It is *good* grief, and the outward tears, if one could look inwardly, would reflect the rainbow of *joy* in my heart. Praying the news of the day, if we do not allow it to impact our emotions, can be a discipline of asking for forgiveness over and over again. "Forgive them, Abba, for they/we know not what they/we do." Can we begin to *see* beyond outward appearances to the depth of beauty, love, and peace that is our real Self and that of everything? While "in defenselessness is our strength" may seem ridiculous by worldly values, it is the Way, the Truth, and the Life that Jesus' own life exemplified. And, as I understand it, defenselessness is one of the basic tenets of the martial arts.

For years, I pondered Jesus' "attack" on the money lenders at the temple, never quite understanding or accepting explanations given in study groups. Then, when at St. Agnes I "attacked" a friend completely conscious of what I was doing, a small glimmer of possible understanding dawned: Each individual living in St. Agnes's rectory had his or her own room upstairs away from the public, the one place we could truly be alone—a mini sacred space. One parishioner, a young friend who knew no boundaries, would simply appear at my door or in my room, expecting special attention regularly. Late one afternoon she arrived, became quite aggressive announcing that she was there to stay whether I liked it or not. Knowing her well, aware that we were alone in the building so I wouldn't embarrass her, I stood up and began shouting, "T. get out of my room! You are never again to come up here without an invitation." I "yelled" her all the way down the stairs as she kept trying to shut me up, fearing someone would hear me.

Even as I "attacked" her, in my mind and heart I was winging her love, I meant her no harm and I felt no guilt. The fruits of this hard expression of love were wonderful and mutual. My acting in a way totally out of character got her attention. She finally began to understand my need for solitude and silence; our friendship continued to grow. I learned that when I was "nice," allowing another to "attack" me, inwardly I, then, attacked myself with resentment and frustration. I realized that having one's space invaded feels, at least to me, like an attack, whether it be a stray dog jumping on me, a telemarketer calling, or a radio blaring away in traffic, we all have our comfort zone with space boundaries. I prayed that my seeming attack had been a wake-up call for T. in much the same spirit as that of a Zen teacher who pokes a distracted disciple on the head. And the ripple effect of love and truth expressed from that one event became other lessons for both of us.

A friend once asked me if I liked a certain word. At the time, I was amused at the idea of liking or not liking particular words. Since then, I have come to appreciate that yes, some words really speak to me more than others. *Atonement* is one such word. I like it because the meaning is there in the word itself: *at-one-ment*. I like it because I resonate to the notion of being at one with everyone and with all of Creation including the Divine Guest abiding in our hearts.

Atonement is at the heart of faith. For Jesus' life, passion, and death on the Cross can be seen and, perhaps, experienced as the reconciliation and a continuing covenant between Love and humankind. This journey we are taking is the way for our at-one-ment with LoveConsciousness. As Simone Weil articulated so well, God reaches out of time and space to take hold of our soul. We need only to say our "yes" to be subdued and won over. Mary is a model for giving consent to the Spirit. Joseph also said his *yes* when he listened to his dreams and took Mary as his wife. What beautiful examples they must have been all of their lives for Jesus. He must have drawn strength from all the *yeses* of his parents on the journey-to-Life roads he traveled. When the time came for his heart-rending prayer in the Garden of Gethsemane, he could voice the *yes* that led to the Cross.

Now once God has received our *yes*, we are not congratulated and taken to the mountaintop. No, all too soon we seem to be left holding the bag, so to speak. God *seems* to abandon us. Mary was left to ponder things in her heart. Hers was a faith that seemed to be free of the guilt and separation that leads to fear. Joseph, it would seem, received his strength and guidance through dreams and a deep, committed faith. Would that we knew more about Joseph 16. Though Jesus had known the absence of God in the desert, he must have felt it most keenly on the Cross. "My God, why have You abandoned me?" Even Jesus, it seems, had to experience the complete absence of Abba, had to know the abyss of emptiness. We share with Jesus in our own desert days and dark nights of the soul, when Love *seems* to have abandoned us completely.

Yet, once having *known* LoveConsciousness and our soul having been sought, nourished, and won, be it ever so fleetingly, the tables are turned. Now we must reach out of time and space searching and groping for the Mystery of Love's way with us. And isn't this a part of our cross? For we now recognize that to be at-one with Love, we must surrender all the world's values and accept that we are One with Love. To deny the upside-down values that ego-illusions hold dear and to extend the Love we are is to live in the Real world, where we know Love as It simply *is*. As we Awaken on these roads that Jesus knew so well, we participate in more and more moments of the Beloved's loving companion Presence with and within us.

Just as Jesus stood accused, recognizing, feeling, and forgiving the transgressions of the Soul of the world, we are invited to share in one another's burdens—not as martyrs usually, but as lovers silently offering ourselves in prayer and service into the Heart of Love. To be in *at-one-ment* calls us to be hidden saints in the world, to be grateful and utterly vulnerable. Dependent only on God, *at-one-ment* brings forgiveness and sets us free to trust one another; to let go. Then, we really begin to know Who and Whose we are.

As we experience Oneness with the Source of our being and acknowledge LoveConsciouness as our birthright, we also come to know ourselves as One with the Earth, given as gift into our care for our happiness and well-being.

In some area of our lives, we have all been broken and wounded. Healing comes when we are ready to acknowledge our woundedness, to forgive all that led to our woundedness and through our wounds to share in the wounds of Christ, which is to know the wounds of our sisters and brothers: the woundedness of our world and environment. And inasmuch as we move toward forgiveness, atonement, and reconciliation, we come to understand with the heart's wisdom and to share with LoveConsciousness in the meaning of the Cross, ever an invitation for us to surrender our lives fully into the heart of Love with boundless confidence.

Life's journey is a movement from the passive, where we are first called and loved, to a full, mature spirituality where we come to love with abandon; where we are able to surrender ourselves into Love's hands without reserve. Charles de Foucauld is one who surrendered himself utterly to God. His prayer of abandonment is a prayer of the heart. Having prayed it morning and night (and sometimes in between) for about twenty-five years, I can attest that it is a prayer of power, a prayer to discover where the resistances of our minds and hearts dwell. Whereas Charles de Foucauld prayed it to the Father, I pray it to the Heart of my heart, the Beloved. One must find his or her own name for the Unnamable. I share this prayer with you, slightly revised:

> *(Beloved),*
> *I abandon myself into your hands;*
> *do with me what You will.*
> *Whatever You may do, I thank You.*
> *I am ready for all, I accept all.*
> *Let only your Will be done in me,*
> *and in all your creatures—*
> *I wish no more than this, (my Friend).*
>
> *Into your hands I commend my soul;*
> *I offer it to You with all the love of my heart.*
> *For I love You,*
> *and so need to give myself,*
> *to surrender myself into your hands*
> *without reserve*
> *and with boundless confidence,*
> *for You are (the Beloved of my heart, the Life of my life.)*

Father Edward J. Farrell, who introduced this prayer to me, used it in retreats around the world with hundreds of individuals. Like many others, I have found that my resistances change from time to time. One line may seem natural and easy for a time, then I seem to choke on it at other times. For me, it has been the single most powerful prayer of my life. Whether I pray it out of gratitude and praise, or whether I am in the throes of grief, I sense Love's presence and am lifted up each time I offer my soul in abandonment.

I once asked for a guiding dream on "the road to Jerusalem" at a time of great loneliness in my life when I was questioning my understanding of "passion." The dream: I was at a conference/seminar where one participant spoke briefly about having discovered what passion meant in his life. I felt bereft because I didn't know what real passion was. I felt that I was looking old, so I fastened clips on my eyelids and knees to pull up the wrinkles. Not realizing that I looked ridiculous, I went to get approval for my efforts. My friend just looked bewildered by my bizarre efforts to be young: as if to ask, who would bother with such a farce? He loved me unconditionally as I was, teaching me that passion is not an ego-related romantic obsession.

This seemingly petty dream embarrassed me enough to get my attention. I realized that my limited understanding of passion was fraught with *personalism* and *emotionalism*. The dream also awakened me to ponder the meaning of how unworthy and unlovable I was feeling; as if I had to somehow work to make myself desirable. I was buying into the ego-illusions of worldly values. Fear was still very much alive in me. Having been distracted from the "narrow road," with the loving guidance of many, I was led into the land of silence and solitude, centering prayer and meditation, and toward the journey into unconditional Love.

Our dreams can often be catalysts for change and movement in our lives and spiritual development. Yet, this dream had nothing to do with any real understanding of the power of authentic passion. The Passion we associate with Jesus between the night of the Last Supper and his bodily death on the Cross clearly exhibits his unflagging zeal for his mission and the authenticity of the way and the truth of his lived Life at every moment—as Teacher, Servant, Way-Shower—no matter what the circumstance. When I asked myself, "Is there anything I care about enough that I would give my life to or for?" the answer seemed simple: Yes. I am already on the road to the Cross: dying to ego-fear illusions, to all that separates me from extending love, forgiveness, and blessing to the world. Yes. To surrender or abandon myself into Love's hands daily and to offer myself in service as I am led—or even driven—by the Spirit has become my experience of passion. And real passion carries with it deep, abiding peace, gratitude, and gentle joy.

I was taught that Jesus died for our sins and those of the world to save us: We have *only* to believe and we are saved. Yet, doesn't that set us apart from Jesus and his many life-giving teachings? What is the meaning of Jesus' living and dying, if not to teach us how to live as fully, as authentically, and as present to LoveConsciousness as he lived and died? Throughout his life and passing from this world, Jesus as Redeemer taught us the way to release ourselves through the Holy Spirit, helping us forgive all the fear-illusions of sin, of blame and guilt, as well as the mind games the ego would have us believe and live by. I'm not an intellectual, so these theological—God logic—words and the ideas they convey about God/Jesus never took deep root in my psyche. Yet, the authentic Way Jesus lived flowered in me as meaning *our* way, *our* truth, and *our* life toward wholeness—if we would only follow the journey he took to a Life of loving Service in every thought, word, and deed.

The "I Ams" of Jesus continue to be both blessing and challenge for me. Each one seems to be an invitation to delve deeper into the Mystery of Jesus' unconditional Love for us. I've come to believe that when Jesus said to us, "You are the light of the world," he was calling us to live fully into his "I Ams." A powerful "exercise" is to ponder and meditate on each of the "I Ams": "I am a true Vine." "I am the Way," "the Truth and the Life." "I am an open Door." "I am Bread of Life." "I am a good Shepherd." "I am the light of the world." "I am the resurrection and the life." Taking each one into silence and prayer from time to time, you may find them imprinting your heart, surprising you with insights, and flowing through your life as lived experience.

Jesus' imperatives, "Choose life!" "Fear not!" "You are the light of the world!" "These things I do, you will do—and more!" "Love your enemies!" "I come so you may have life in abundance!" are terse phrases that can set the heart on Fire. Thus, can passion begin to bud. The temptations clearly point out that Jesus did not come to save us so that we have only to believe in Him to be saved. Jesus is the Way-shower to well-being, to forgiveness and healing, to authentic Life. To walk these roads that Jesus walked in our own unique way offering our gifts can lead us to our passion/Passion. And we die, we die to all that separates us from Life, from living into the full potential you already are in essence beyond the fears, ignorance, and ego-illusions lurking in the shadow.

To walk the road to Jerusalem takes on a timely, potentially wondrous or disastrous dimension today. So much hatred and violence will only beget more of the same. LoveConsciousness is always the answer beyond the world's ways. Jerusalem, a new Jerusalem, has the unparalleled opportunity to become one of the greatest portals of spiritual energy and Power in the world, a melding of the three peoples of the Book arising from the same origins: the Jewish, Muslim, and Christian faiths open to and welcoming all. To recognize and affirm the tapestry, similar histories, the mosaic of varying traditions and aspirations rather than our present focus on yesterday's hatreds and the unending conflicts of old could revolutionize that part of the world. Jerusalem could become a spiritual Center for all people, all religions.

When will the world learn that to attack others in thought, word, or deed is simply to attack ourselves? War and violence can only beget more war and violence at a terrible cost: depleting resources of energy, death, and maiming of untold lives and psyches, and financial devastation to millions. History, if not commonsense, is proof of this truth. Conversely, forgiveness and peace will beget more forgiveness and peace with mutual blessing, hope, and communion in return.

What could it mean for the peoples of the world to choose to walk these roads, to consciously choose Life, not as a religion, but for the well-being of the planet and each individual on it? Wars would have to become obsolete; prisons would be mostly empty. All the wondrous tapestry of peoples and nations would share and thrive in a spirit of co-creation, co-operation, and community. A passion for healing the earth would foster a return to pure air, pure water, renewing the earth scars, monitoring global uses of resources; education, religion, health, financial matters, and all manner of social institutions would include the arts, cultural diversity, beauty, mutuality, respect, encouragement, spirituality. We would evolve from death-oriented cultures to life giving, celebrating, naturally ritualistic grateful peoples.

Recently, I was filled with hope and joy as I absorbed every word Al Gore spoke in an interview by Charlie Rose. Tears of gratitude welled up as he shared *so passionately* about the planetary crises upon us. I wept with tears of relief hearing him speak out. Whenever tears arise spontaneously, whether in beauty, a magnificent performance, a service of Love, or, here, in listening and noting Al Gore's passion for and commitment to the earth, I *know* that I am witnessing something of truth. Though the plight of our planet home may, indeed, be *an inconvenient truth,*[16] I pray that humanity will arise to meet and act on this crucial challenge with creativity, ingenuity, dedication, and a passion that leads to the renewal and healing of our home.

Jesus' baptism by water and the Spirit led him to the desert, where he came face to face with his innermost being, an initiation into his earthly mission. Jesus' journey to Jerusalem and death on the Cross was a baptism by Fire, an initiation into eternal Life and cosmic Christ Consciousness. Jesus shared everything he possibly could with us. In embarking on this journey with full consciousness, we may begin to see with our inner spiritual eyes and to listen and hear with our inner spiritual ears, almost as if we were with Peter, James, and John, sharing Jesus' total glory at the Transfiguration; we may be able to sense Jesus' agony in the Garden alone; or, his loneliness, possible disappointment, and fatigue as he was all but abandoned by his disciples. We may find ourselves expressing gratitude for his teachings, his life, and his ongoing Presence with us. Jesus will never abandon us no matter how far we may choose to separate ourselves with fear and ego-illusions.

By his life mission, his words, and his ever-authentic responses to all of life, we have been given a road map to Love and Light and Power. Truly, by the choices we make, we can become active, love-filled co-creators giving birth to a new, life-giving, peace-filled world. Or we can participate in hanging onto the present diseased, and dying world filled with fear and living "yesterday's will of God." The choice is always ours. Each one of us makes a choice, one way or another.

What clearer message do we need that we can take the same pilgrimage: living with that same vulnerability, openness, compassion, and authenticity to ourselves, to our neighbors all over the globe, to our earth home, and to the Heart of all hearts? For without this journey to the Cross, without this journey of surrender to Love and dying to our ego-false selves, we will not easily find ourselves on the road to Emmaus—and joy.

7

The Road to Emmaus

*I*magine that you walked with Jesus two thousand years ago, that you knew the loving authority of Jesus' presence. You were also a witness, albeit from afar, to the tortures inflicted upon Jesus by those of earthly power. You experienced the terrifying darkness when the sun was veiled and the skies cried out with thunder and lightning as earth quaked and groaned in response to Love's crucifixion on the Cross. Yet, we can see from Jesus' crucifixion that the death of the body always portends a new birth, an open door. Here birthed from Jesus' life and teachings, a new energy, a new way of relating to the Creator, creation, and to one another was given expression. Jesus' life pointed to a way to live so completely in Abba's abundant and eternal love, that we, too, can see our potential to express our holiness and wholeness that we are when fear no longer separates us from our true being. Although Jesus' death may seem then to have silenced his Voice, the Good News has only grown stronger, though not without much conflict along the way and we discover on this road that Jesus is with us always.

What might dwell in you as you recall the pregnant silent void in the days that followed Jesus' physical death? What concerns might you have had? Would doubt and fear have overwhelmed your hopes and faith? Then, when you hear of Jesus' reappearance to some of the disciples, what might have been evoked in you?

Take time now, if you wish, to reenter the story. Imagine that you are walking toward Emmaus with a friend recalling Jesus' life with you, when a stranger joins you. You can't believe that he is so ignorant to all that has transpired. So, you and your friend relate everything you can recall of Jesus' death and disappearance from the tomb. You tell him of the women who saw a vision of angels saying that Jesus is alive. Then, unexpectedly, this stranger turns the table and quotes to you from all the prophets concerning Christ—even telling you that it was *necessary* for Christ to suffer. How do you respond as you walk and talk with this stranger who now seems such a paradox?

As you near your home, the stranger seems to be going on farther. What does it mean that you persuade him to stay? Are you merely being gracious because of the late hour and the need to eat? When at table together, he breaks the bread and blesses it; when he gives it to you to eat, almost immediately, you recognize Jesus. What a moment! What a breath of overwhelming joy! Then, just as mysteriously as Jesus appeared, he vanishes from your sight.

Do you believe with your eyes, or, is it the burning love imprinted on your heart that assures you that Jesus has truly risen from the dead, that Jesus is, indeed, a living Presence, a Reality in your life? There seems to be only one response possible. You run out to find your friends to tell them. Can you imagine what their response might be to hear, but not experience, such extraordinary news?

Imagining ourselves in the Good News story is one way to evoke recollections of Christ's presence in our own lives today. Have you ever met and known Jesus on an Emmaus road? How do you experience God's presence in your life? We know a triune God. For through Jesus, we can come to know God with many different names and faces, a Presence with whom we can commune. And through Jesus, we have been sent the Holy Spirit, the Comforter, to be present with us always. What aspect of the Trinity are you most familiar with, or most uncomfortable? To whom do you pray? Have you ever known the Oneness of Light and Love? Most likely, we have all had Emmaus moments, times or events that seem beyond any worldly explanation. Sometimes, you only realize such a Gift many years later as in the following blessing that came into my life.

I was in the process of moving from four years living alone on twenty-four acres of woods and meadow near Lake Huron in Michigan—a healing, heavenly haven—to a one-room apartment in Vermont. Two days before the movers were to arrive, they called to announce they could *only* make the delivery on Thanksgiving Day and they would require a bank check or cash. I was ill with what turned out to be pneumonia, the family was away, I didn't know anyone, and my only bank account was at Merrill Lynch in Burlington, which, with my not knowing the territory, seemed really far away.

Early the morning before Thanksgiving I presented myself looking down and out, I'm sure, with a runny nose, teary eyes, and coughing continuously. I can hardly blame the receptionist for backing away and wanting only to see me out of there. In my naiveté I asked where the tellers were located; I explained I needed a bankers check for moving fees. In fact, I probably told her much more than she'd ever need or want to know. I was miserable, lonely, and felt desperate. She explained that there was no way I could get a check that day. I knew that I had a financial adviser, but had never met or talked to him. So, I insisted that he be advised of my need.

I waited for what seemed ages noting that the other two customers were sitting as far away from me as possible. Feeling powerless and bereft, I was close to tears. Then, the front door opened and in walked a dapper old gentleman, dressed as if he were going to the opera, sporting a bowler hat. He walked directly over and stood right in front of me. With a sweep of his hat, he bowed to me looking into my eyes, and then walked toward the door to leave. Turning his head back toward me, he gave a slight bow and said, "Have a grand day." Then, he simply disappeared. Within a short time, a woman arrived with some papers for me to sign and I was on my way with the needed check.

All the way home I marveled at the encounter with this unknown "angel." I still felt physically miserable; yet, it was as if I had had a special blessing. My heart kept welling up with a gentle joy; it was a gray day that matched how my body felt; yet, it still seemed as if the sun were shining. Although I don't know who this stranger was, I do know that such moments are holy moments filled with wonder and surprise. I treasure them as Emmaus greetings on this journey we are all making alone, yet very much together as One.

Each of us is a capacity for God. Each of us experience and reflect the Divine uniquely, in a way unlike any other. For much of my life, I feared the God of the Hebrew Scripture. The *Thou shalt nots* were the essence of my earliest conscious experience of God as Father. Yet, at a deep, barely conscious level, I must have known and loved God as Creator, the Giver of breath and life. The wind was always a special friend that whispered to me of freedom as my open arms welcomed its embrace. And the wind spoke also of power, especially during the great hurricane of 1936 that uprooted trees, washed away the beach front and humbled us to nights of candlelight when I was five years old. I was in awe of this friend and I loved her.

One of the most profound movements in my own spiritual formation has been to discern evermore clearly the various ways that Love lives in me—my own Emmaus moments. As I share a few of them, you are invited to recall some of those times that you have discovered yourself on the road to Emmaus. When our hearts burn with the Love of Divine Presence, a deep gratitude wells up. Sometimes we hold these in our hearts as a hidden gift, at other times, we feel compelled to share these precious moments with another or others.

Other friends, rocks and stones, communicated solidarity and firmness in life; what is more, like the pieces of wood and shells I gathered, *life* was in them. Each unique piece of earth came with a message that seemed special to me. I embraced trees, made secret rooms in bushes, lived in trees, captured insects and sea life to admire; I tried to envelop the ocean in my arms, imitated the birds, told the stars my dreams, and I laid in beds of leaves in the fall and in snow in the winter. I was in ecstasy with the arrival of each new season. The earth became my Mother, my teacher, my companion, the heavens and all I could imagine beyond were my Father. I knew without doubt that Love/Spirit abided in this natural world; I did not know then that Love/Spirit abided in me, in all.

Over the years, I have come to experience and call God by many names besides Creator: Strength . . . Great Mystery . . . Nameless One . . . Light . . . . I am deeply touched by the Creation story, our call, privilege, capacity, and responsibility to be good tenders of our earth. Over the decades, I have had many positive responses of awe, wonder, praise, and gratitude toward Creator God, as well as more negative emotions of fearing God's judgment and authority. In growing up with what came across as a one-sided, patriarchal Yahweh, I felt disconnected, and distanced myself from God as Father-Judge-Authority.

A beginning reconciliation with God as Father came out of a conversation with my own father, who I experienced as a dictatorial judgmental figure some of the time throughout my childhood. During a vacation with my parents when I was in my fifties, we were recollecting humorous, and sometime regrettable, scenes from our lives together. Then, out of the blue, Dad asked me, "Did I do right in insisting that you become a librarian if I was to help put you through college? I've always wondered about that." In truth, I had carried resentment about that for over thirty years. Yet, I was surprised to hear myself say, "Well, I was really more interested in psychology and religion; yet, having library training has helped me in more ways that I can count. And, when I chose later to follow my continued interest in other areas, I was far more mature and prepared." Somehow, out of that brief interaction, an unspoken forgiveness lifted this unexpressed weight from both of us. Regrettably, too many of us carry around such unneeded burdens for much of our lives. And usually, we do not realize how tied our image and relationship with God, as Father, is to our experiences with our natural father. And, what joy to be reconciled [with the Father/father].

Another way I have come to appreciate the "Old Testament God" is in coming to know the God of history, God speaking through the Prophets, God's covenant. My awakening to God's call to social justice came from one of today's prophets, Daniel Berrigan. Even though I had very much felt the pain of injustice and oppression for as long as I can remember, I seemed to have been paralyzed by fear-filled feelings of powerlessness that kept me from action before meeting Dan.

For the first four of five seminars with him at the Guild For Spiritual Guidance,[17] I simply cried. He spoke words that my heart had long known, yet which I had never been able to articulate with such clarity. Though what he said was clearly gospel, I'm sure I could have heard him if he'd been saying, fish for sale, or even if he had not uttered a word.

Each time I meet someone whose life is a *living*, authentic witness to Truth, I cry. I seem to be faced with a choice: I can turn away and avoid the risk of being led to a "place I would rather not go," or I can choose to remain open and vulnerable. I shall ever be grateful that I had the privilege of being with Dan and others who walk through their lives with such purpose, passion, clarity, and integrity. Since then, I see Love at work on the Emmaus road in so many of today's prophets. I have lived into the call to be more in solidarity with those who seem to be powerless in our society, I aspire to live my life with more passion and integrity. And never has my joy and gratitude been greater: all, with thanks to the wisdom and guidance of so many friends and colleagues living here or in the unseen realm of Love, as well as the ever-available counsel of Love's Voice in our hearts.

The Psalms have ever been for many a great source of inspiration, comfort, and a way of knowing God. I memorized many as a child and loved their beauty and form. However, I was always appalled by the negativity of so many: causing havoc to enemies; smiting whole nations. In fifth and sixth grades, our school day began with one of the pupils reading a Psalm in front of the class. I was always excited to choose the Psalm I would read; yet, I dreaded standing before everyone reading in my quavering voice with knees shaking. Inevitably, I would have decided on one of my favorites and then read Psalm 117, the shortest Psalm.

Starting in the early 1970s as I would ponder the Psalms, new words began to arise spontaneously making them more timely and meaningful to me until, as some of you may know, *Psalms For Praying* was birthed in 1996, something I had not anticipated. In this way, I discovered a new depth of how God meets us on the road to Emmaus. This twenty-or-so years' Labor of Love changed my concept and relationship to God: as Friend and as a living and loving companion Presence, I discovered Love as the Beloved of my heart, the Beloved of all hearts . . . Life of my life, Breath of my breath, Heart of my heart. Psalm 101 is an example:

> *I will sing of loyalty and of*
> *justice;*
> *to You, O Beloved, I will sing.*
> *I will give heed to the way that*
> *leads to peace.*
> *O, come make your home*
> *in my heart.*
>
> *I would walk with integrity of heart*
> *in all I do.*
> *And look in all things for your*
> *Face.*
>
> *May I be a reflection of your Love*
> *to those who go astray.*
> *May I reflect the freedom of your*
> *Truth, and*
> *become a beneficial presence*
> *in the world.*
>
> *Forgive me, O Merciful One, if I turn*
> *from a neighbor in need.*
> *Humble me if I become arrogant*
> *and greedy.*
> *Enwrap me in your Presence.*

I seek the company of those who
love You,
that I may grow in wisdom;
I enter into the Silence, into your
dwelling place,
And listen for your Word.

For, no one who oppresses another,
who keeps company with injustice,
will dwell in the house of Love.
And, no one who walks in darkness
will know the glory of Light.

In the morning offer yourself in
prayer,
by night surrender to Love
in trust;
For those who walk in the Light
with grateful hearts,
will radiate peace to the world.

One of the most difficult ways we come to know God is when we seem to lose the sense of God's presence—when we feel totally abandoned. At such a time of great darkness in my life, I had been unable to pray, seemingly paralyzed with emptiness and grief. Recently separated, I was alone at home one winter's evening. While sitting on the couch barely aware of the snowstorm beating at the window, I wept into the Silence. After a long time, the sobs abated and anger welled up within from the depths of despair. For the second time in my life, I cried aloud to God, "You promised You would not give us more than we can bear. This is my limit. Please do something!" Then I covered my face with my hands and the tears continued to flow, yet with no accompanying sobs.

In less than two minutes, I heard a soft noise at the window and turned to look. There on the outside sill sat a most beautiful white dove seemingly oblivious to the storm. Even though I thought this "could not be," there she was just Be-ing there for me. We "communed" with one another for maybe three minutes. I closed my eyes in a prayer of gratitude for the peace and love which now enveloped me. When I opened them, though the visitation had ended, the dove's imprint was still on the window and continues to live inside me. Sometimes, as I sit in the Silence, I smile in wonder at the infinite variety of ways that Love creates to knock at the door of our soul, to love and to comfort us in our sorrow, to surprise us with new Life. The *Emmaus moments* come when we most need them or least expect them.

Through rainbows, I became aware of how the Beloved continues to covenant with us. In a three-month period, I was blessed by rainbows, real and artificial. One rainbow "followed" me from a town where my son was taking his driving test, home again, and then to work about thirty miles farther, a period of well over an hour. Another time, when I was grieving, I saw the first full rainbow I had ever seen, a clearly defined arc over the ocean, from horizon to horizon. As I watched with wonder until it faded away, I distinctly heard the words, "I promise you joy." I carried those words in my heart during the painful years to come.

The first New Year's Eve I ever spent alone, I decided to draw my loneliness and sadness. To my surprise, I drew a beautiful rainbow and wrote the word JOY, a renewed promise for the New Year. My mourning lessened; joy peeked into my life. These rainbow glimpses of promised joy culminated after *seven* years. I was alone at prayer one morning in the chapel of St. Agnes in Detroit, where I had come to live and minister as a lay volunteer. The chapel was suddenly filled with rainbow light that seemed to end at the small altar. I heard the words, *You have lived into the joy I promised you.* Though I knew it was true, I was still tempted to think that it had been my imagination, until at liturgy that afternoon someone prayed in gratitude for the morning rainbow that seemed to end right in the chapel window. Emmaus is anywhere we are when Love comes to call.

As a child, I was expected to get up and go to the Holy Name Episcopal Church for the 9:30 service followed by Sunday School. I enjoyed it and, in time, came to feel connected to "Something More." Yet, I sensed something was missing when I talked with my Catholic friends. I had been "encouraged" to stay away from anyone who was different from us. I endured the pain this brought, ignored the suggestions, and felt burdened with guilt for this parental bias, which I came to understand as prejudice, something I couldn't understand.

I can clearly recall at about ten, walking to St. John's church with Sally Bartlett, a neighborhood friend. She told me a big lie; then she explained that she was on her way to confession and she couldn't think of anything she'd done wrong, so she could now confess this lie. This was a major revelation. So often I felt like I was a "miserable sinner" and what a relief it would be to tell someone about my sins and get forgiven for them.

When Sally made the signing of the cross—another revelation. At home that night, I created a nun's veil with a towel draped over my head; I confessed to "her" in the mirror and then let "her" forgive me: creative and surprisingly helpful, a relief of sorts. Then, I stood in front of the mirror and practiced *crossing* myself. Quite often after absorbing what for me were wondrous new insights, I felt drawn to venture on to St. John's after Sunday School. I would sneak in the door to a back pew, and listen to the Mass in Latin. It was pure mystery.

Over the years I began to experience the signing of the cross as a powerful image of how I feel the Presence working in me: touching the forehead evokes for me God as Creator, as Light, Mind—touching the heart, I sense Jesus as LoveConsciousness, Friend, Indwelling Divine Guest, Beloved of my heart. And, touching each shoulder, I know the Holy Spirit as Divine Counselor, Fire, as the Activator who sends me out to share myself wherever I am sent, wherever I am, with whomever I meet.

My litany for the holy is changing and maturing evermore deeply within me. Though Christianity is my birth home, I feel comfortable and find wisdom in most denominations and religions, but never in extremism. I *am* concerned with fundamentalism or fanaticism in any religion. These seem to be so biased and based on fear that, in time, some form of attack seems likely. Jesus' life was filled with humor, friendship with all, wisdom of the ages. Jesus' *simple* witness through his life and teachings, his clarity about the spirit of the Law, resonate with me as the only authentic *evangelism* we have, the essence of all we are invited to discover on all the roads that he walked.

Through journaling, we have an open book to our souls, to our growth and growing edges, our Emmaus moments, or as a record to reread from time to time: a plumb line to help discern where we are on the Journey. I offer a few examples from my journal entries when I was living in Detroit, for possible insights to your own way of journaling or simply as catalysts for pondering.

February: I don't think my life made much of a difference to anyone today, a sad feeling. Who was I Eucharist to? Who did I encourage? Love? Help? Be a friend to? I feel like a stranger in a strange land. And yet, You gifted me with your Presence in so many ways! Why do You not give up on me?

Marvin opened my heart this morning. The doorbell rang early and I opened the door to a shivering, sad-eyed man who had been out for three days and nights in this below freezing weather, living in abandoned cars. His lips were purple and he was shivering so hard he could barely speak. Giving him the warmth of simple food, the hope of finding shelter, and a bit of friendship warmed my heart. A good man, a simple man with no family, who was not going to give up hoping, even though he had lost his job two weeks ago when the company moved. It could break one's heart. Yet, because of his endurance, perseverance, faith, and gratitude where bitterness could lie, I am heartened and humbled. Marvin shows me how Jesus calls us to a faith-filled, vulnerable sharing of our selves with others in Love.

A friend and I drove Marvin to a shelter where he remained for two weeks. The next time I heard from him was when he appeared again at the door. This time he had come to offer some time to volunteer in gratitude for having been received. "And one turned back to give thanks." Perhaps we had traveled Emmaus Road together for a short time.

I see nothing, and suddenly it is good, this not knowing. Christ seems to be stripping my soul bare, making a clear, clean space for a new creation in me. And so I get down on my hands and knees, utilizing this emptying-out scrubbing floors, hiding the painful searing of purifying Flame. Yet, I still do not accept your Fire with the grace I aspire to. Yes, I wrestle with You, my Friend, even knowing and hoping that in the end You alone will have your way in me and with me.

Later . . . a dream of a heart of flame held out to me with the simple words, "You are the light of the world!" I am deeply moved by this dream. Then, busy from dawn until early evening, not a minute to rest. I shall never forget the sheer shock etched on Mildred's face as she faithfully entered into prayer while we waited. The heroic attempt to save Jerome's life was a fleeting respite in which we could hope. He passed on, salt of the earth returning to the earth and new Life. Watching with Mildred, I sensed the Loving Presence accompanying Jerome and with all those gathered there together. The Emmaus Road is a gentle witness to Life even in the midst of physical dying. A grace to be there.

. . . Another incredibly full day of not doing anything planned, so why plan? Brought soup, bread, and dessert to Mildred and family. I am moved by her gifted grandchildren, by the support and endurance of her faith and that of her whole family. A strong sense of Jesus' presence as I drove along the highway. Just the two of us enjoying one another a gentle, peaceful time which was good . . . another Emmaus grace!

Emmaus is whenever we are Awake and can see through our inner eyes and hear with our inner ears. When we know our forgiveness and live knowing the Divine Guest residing within our heart.

Most of my responses to meeting Jesus, the Christ, are positive. I am ever grateful for all Jesus' invitations: to love and serve; to justice and compassion; to humility; to weep with others and to share in their joy; to be a pray-er; to welcome new life and Awakening consciousness; to forgiveness; to live our lives to fullest potential. Yet, one stumbling block was for many years the "be ye perfect" injunction. That was put to rest when I learned that the translation could as easily and more appropriately read, "be ye *whole* or *holy.*"

When I read the following, while studying *A Course in Miracles* even further insights emerged. "To the extent to which you value guilt, to that extent will you perceive a world in which attack is justified. To the extent to which you recognize guilt is meaningless, to that extent you will perceive attack cannot be justified. This is in accord with perception's fundamental law" (*ACIM* 25, III, 1). Jesus exemplifies this with the woman about to be stoned. He always chooses a loving response rather than attack modes. To feel guilty is to be in ego-fear.

Jesus invites us all to join in the Dance of life with one another and our loving Companion Friend. Writing or telling our own unique story on the roads Jesus walked with all our joys and sorrows; stumbling and maturing in Love; and facing our ego-fears are powerful steps toward new Life, to being in the world but not of it, to freedom and great gratitude, to abiding peace and gentle inner joy. This is what I experience the journey into Love to be about.

For several decades I have pondered how to envision a balance of masculine and feminine energies within my understanding of Love with us. Not being an intellect or deep thinker, I've traveled through life as what might be characterized as an off-the-chart intuitive. This has certainly been an imbalance, sometimes with a loss of credibility. For instance, when a man once approached me at a book signing for *Psalms for Praying* and asked me for all the sources that I had based the book on so he could translate the book into Hebrew, I was truly befuddled. When I shared that each Psalm was simply the result of prayer and meditation, listening deeply in the silence, and wrestling as a kind of dialogue between two ages, he shook his head dismissively and walked away. Recently, however, while attending a weekend gathering of the Guild for Spiritual Guidance, the presenter, Sister Meg,[18] asked me exactly the same question and received a similar response. She asked if we could get together so she could better understand. As usual, I could only offer simple stories much as those I am sharing with you. When the rest of her lectures included stories from her own experience that reflected the well-thought-through ideas she was presenting, we were all deeply moved. The balance of her intellect, her intuition, and her immediate willingness and capability to respond to our need was a joy to behold.

Whereas my dreams, poetry, journaling, and dialoguing with an issue usually help me to deepen my understanding of Scripture or of any concern, another intuitive form, drawing, often opens new doors. As I travel the roads that Jesus walked, I yearned to delve into a deeper understanding of the Trinity, how the feminine energy fits into this masculine "model." And to be honest, the Dove descending upon Jesus' head at his Baptism never quite resonated in me as an answer to the patriarchal imbalance that I experienced, feminine though it may appear. Then one day, after years of studying and writing on this subject, a double triune in the symbol of the Star of David "fell" into place. Even now, I continue to "play and pray" over the following two "models," as I am, continued works in process, as diagramed:

These well may be naive ponderings on my journey into wholeness as I seek to solve a mystery that needs only to be lived moment by moment. Yet, what these models represent for me is a greater sense of energetic balance that brings seeming opposites together in the Oneness of Love, and in my own soul. Our humanness is ever intersecting with the Divine. The more conscious we become of these dynamics, literally working in and with us, the more Creativity and Intuition may grace us with their gifts. These symbols also place each one of us into the center as the bearers of this wondrous experience we call life. We carry both masculine and feminine energies materially and spiritually. How we extend them out to the world is by the choices we make. When in balance, we are living in the Center radiating Love and Light, which extends out to all we meet. William Blake describes our purpose so simply: "We are set here on Earth for but a short while to learn to bear the beams of Love." At the Center of each model, we are immersed in Love on our pilgrimage along all the roads we travel even as the trinity of Jesus, Mary, and Joseph followed their way to Love.

My first real introduction to Mary came unexpectedly many years ago. A spiritual companion encouraged me to pray to Mary

Star of David

Divine Father—Masculine Principle—Creator of the Universe

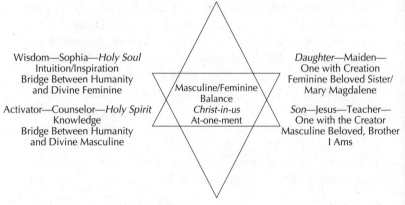

Wisdom—Sophia—*Holy Soul*
Intuition/Inspiration
Bridge Between Humanity
and Divine Feminine

Activator—Counselor—*Holy Spirit*
Knowledge
Bridge Between Humanity
and Divine Masculine

Masculine/Feminine
Balance
Christ-in-us
At-one-ment

Daughter—Maiden—
One with Creation
Feminine Beloved Sister/
Mary Magdalene

Son—Jesus—Teacher—
One with the Creator
Masculine Beloved, Brother
I Ams

Divine Mother—Feminine Principle—Progenitor of the Earth Matrix (Mary)

Equal-sided—Cross

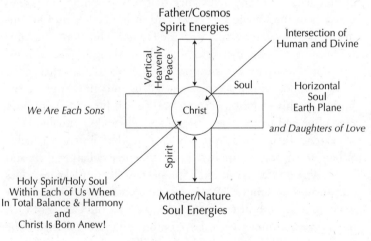

Father/Cosmos
Spirit Energies

Intersection of
Human and Divine

Vertical
Heavenly
Peace

Soul

Horizontal
Soul
Earth Plane

We Are Each Sons

Christ

and Daughters of Love

Spirit

Holy Spirit/Holy Soul
Within Each of Us When
In Total Balance & Harmony
and
Christ Is Born Anew!

Mother/Nature
Soul Energies

(notwithstanding I was not yet of the Catholic faith) in order to discover the hidden Mary in me. He suggested that Mary could help me learn more about the meaning of love. When praying did not have much effect, I decided to try to dialogue with Mary. Naively, without too much expectation of success, I prepared myself in silence until I felt receptive and ready to listen.

Nan: I'd like to talk with you, Mary. I've been told that you might help me understand Love in a deeper way.

Mary: Just out of the blue, you come to me and want to know Love as I knew it. You really do not want to know that kind of pain, my dear.

Nan: Well, I do not want to open your wounds. But, I really do need help. I am already in pain!

Mary: You do not really know what pain is, my dear. I am not belittling the "agony" you have undergone. But do you think *that* in any way compares with seeing your son, your beloved child from the womb, scourged and spit upon and dragged as an animal to a gruesome, humiliating, brutal, nailed-to-wood death between common wretches?

Nan: I'm sorry, Mary. Oh God, how weak and superficial "I'm sorry" sounds!

Mary: I do not say this to mock you. I say it to put your love in perspective. I loved my son as much as any mother on earth. I felt his mission from the beginning. I was blessed beyond words throughout my confinement and even the birth was one of exaltation. My expectations were high because my joy was so great. You, too, have known fleeting joy; you have had high expectations. Your children are blessings to you, too. From his early days my son troubled my heart. He was different from other children and a mother fears this difference; this did not seem a blessing to me. I could not understand such wisdom, such authority; and, you must remember, I did not know then that Jesus, my son, *was* the Chosen One. I believed that I was chosen, in a way, to bear my child in such joy, to have such an understanding man to stand beside me, to have a son who was respected in the Temple circles. Still, as a mother inwardly senses the destiny of her beloved offspring, I tell you in my hidden heart, I cried and despaired from his early years on.

Nan: You sound as if you still carry that despair.

Mary: No, of course not, my dear. You are projecting your feelings. I am telling you of my life as it was then. I was like other mothers in many ways. I bragged about my children; I was proud and far from the perfect saint the years have made me. Yet, that is good. Humanity needs models of perfection to emulate. There are far too few of spiritual dimension in your present world.

Nan: How well we know! Is there more you could tell me about love?

Mary: The hardest part. Are you sure you want to hear it?

Nan: No, but tell me anyway.

Mary: You are such a character. You often say *no*, but sit ready to hear. When you say *yes*, you sometimes go away and close your ears.

Nan: I'm afraid you are right. I *do* want to hear what you tell me. I am slow to learn, but it usually gets through. Oh Mary, I hope it does.

Mary: What you find difficult to hear is the part of Love that demands surrender. This does not mean surrender of your personality so that it merges with another so that you become muted. To surrender to Love at the highest level means totally giving yourself into God's hands. When my son gave his spirit back to the Father, it was the greatest act of faith the universe had ever known. I stood there and felt the impact of the future being born. Love became conscious surrender to the Alpha and Omega for all time. Yet, you miss the point if you expect Christ to do this for you. You, too, need to surrender your heart and soul to Abba, and Christ is the open Door. Christ leads you to Abba. You are coming to that awareness, but you need to take the next step. TRUST totally in the Love of God.

This dialogue with Mary was a blessed turning point. I cried as if my heart would break—and, it did. It broke open and a lifetime of unacknowledged grief spewed forth. My heart's soil, hardened by years of repressed fears, cracked open and was softened by tears of relief and regret. And, I believe, seeds of love long dormant were activated in the light and warmth conveyed by Mary's words to me. Humbled, I recognized the power of dialogue-prayer. I do not need to question if that was *really* Mary or not; I only know the fruits of the dialogue have been life-changing. Life is so full of Mystery. And, what joy we find in living into the Mystery and trusting the Process as we walk on the Emmaus road.

To live the mystery of our own lives as faithfully as Mary lived into the mystery of hers is one of the great challenges of our birthright. A part of Mary's mystery is the Magnificat, an unending source of inspiration. If you have not already done so, writing your own magnificat can be a powerful prayer, a promise to live into. Each time I re-read my own magnificat, which came during a time of meditation many years ago, I renew my aspiration to live into the fullest potential of who I am called to be: Beloved, Heart of my heart, my soul rejoices in You, and my spirit yearns to walk in your ways all the days of my life. I am a woman who aspires to total surrender to your Love in me; I am a woman who struggles and build walls that keep me from receiving all that you would give to me; yet, I am a woman who knows that in reality, I am only Yours.

I listen to your Voice whispering in my ear and echoing in my heart, *I am with you always; I love you; I am yours, you are Mine. As you walk through the sorrows and joys of each day, remember that I am with you always.*

Beloved, You know I am also a woman who forgets. I pray never to lose the knowledge of your Loving Companion Presence, especially in those times that I become fearful and stray from You in my thoughts, words, and deeds. Help me, O Heart of my heart, that I, like Mary, may cry out to You with all my soul: "*Be it done unto me according to your Word.*" Amen.

One cannot easily speak of Mary without the Rosary coming to mind. One does not need to be Catholic to enjoy the serenity, strength, and blessings that can come from this special way of praying. I have come to sense Mary as the feminine model that I aspire to become. Her gentleness, fidelity, grace, peace, and compassion as well as her total surrender in faith to God humbles me. One of the most effective ways of praying with Mary arose spontaneously one day when I felt angry and hurt. I began to pray the rosary, asking Mary to bless the individual with whom I felt estranged. And even before I finished the prayer, forgiveness and thoughts of what I could do to reconcile with that person began to well up in me.

Though I have prayed the Rosary in various ways, I continue to "pray and play" my way into what resonates as natural for me. Barbara Erakko Taylor's updated, creative Rosary has been refreshing and you may find it resonates in your heart as well:

> *Holy Mother, full of Love*
> *new Creation is within You,*
> *and blessed is the presence*
> *of your Compassion.*

> *Indwelling Mother,*
> *Holy Womb of Life,*
> *nurture us into the Oneness of Love*
> *and the Mystery of our forgiven-ness.*
> Amen.

Often in the middle of a sleepless night, I find rest in praying the Rosary in combination with the seven *I Ams* of Jesus:

> *Holy Wisdom, full of grace,*
> *Truth lives within you,*
> *blessed are You among us*
> *and blessed is the fruit of your Love,*
> *the Beloved, who says,*

> *I am the true Vine*
> *I am the Way, the Truth, and the Life*

I am the open Door
I am the Bread of Life
I am the good Shepherd
I am the Light of the World
I am the Resurrection and the Life

Blessed Mary, Mother to All,
pray for us now and
at the moment of our
Awakening into new Life.

Amen.

I continue to ponder on each of the *I Ams* as I believe Jesus gave them with an invitation for each one of us to live into them as fully as we can each in his or her way.

Even so, praying the rosary is not a daily part of my life. I struggled to update it to today's world, until September 11, 2001, when I was led to what, for me and many others who are now praying this way, became an answer in the writing of *Peace Planet: Light for the World. Peace Planet* combines a prayer and a photo for each of the world's 198 countries. To pray this book is to hold the world in your hand; an opportunity to meet and pray with and for your neighbors around the world.

The following is excerpted from the preface to the book.

September 11, 2001, will long be remembered as a terrible and shocking tragedy. Forever vivid will be the memory of how our nation and the world began to mourn the loss of lives, and the loss of our innocence as we joined in solidarity with nations and peoples devastated by war and violence. For days I paced and tried to find the words to pray. I felt desolate, powerless, and enormously disheartened. My only solace was to sit in the silence and allow the indwelling Presence to become my prayer.

The answer came when a friend gave me a prayer for peace listing all the countries of the world. As I prayed over each nation every day, I began to experience these countries as friends. Humbled by how little I knew of our global neighbors, I started to locate each nation on a map and read about it. Little by little, *Peace Planet* emerged. It was a prayer response to a worldwide horror.

To stand in prayer-solidarity, committed to peace, has brought deep healing, and an even deeper pledge to spread seeds of peace in the world through prayer and service. We will never know the myriad blessings that have been borne out of these ashes of destruction. The random acts of kindness. The prayers and un-heralded works of mercy. We unfold the story with our actions. Prayer *can* become the undergirding, the foundation, the infra-structure, the power force of peace.[19]

As we travel these roads together, we do well to encourage one another. To keep reminding ourselves of the importance of forgiveness, of the freedom that comes from letting go of the ego-illusions that teach us to fear, of loving *as* we love ourselves, even those who seem to be enemies. Knowing our Oneness with all, who can really be an enemy? For Love and forgiveness have the power and function to overcome all enmities, all fear. Who knows when we will meet Someone on this Emmaus road who will kindle a spark within us and set our heart on fire? Who will recognize when he or she may be in the company of an angel? Love is our greatest strength, and freedom. Unless we open our hearts we may miss the Gift—the One who may be the Stranger walking the way with us.

This brings us to the Road to Galilee, the ordinary time of daily life, where we recognize we are always preparing, often in retrospect, for the next turn of the road, the next challenge, a new lesson, a surprise by the Spirit. To be ever mindful of the Guidance we can call upon helps us to follow more consciously the leadings of the Spirit.

Even when led to unknown territory, to a place we'd rather not go, we are always blessed in wondrous ways, *when* we have sense enough to stay out of the way and to trust the Process of Love working in and through us. At least, this has ever been my experience; I pray it be so for you, too, dear friends.

8

❧

The Road to Galilee

Galilee is of Hebrew origin meaning "ring" or "circuit," and is descriptive of a ring of cities around the hill country where Jesus' ordinary life was spent. Here, Jesus gathered disciples, taught them and all who came to hear him the way of forgiveness and Love rather than living with fear, guilt, a sense of sinfulness, and ego's illusionary desires as companions. Always careful to remain at One with the Spirit and centered in Love, Jesus would often slip away for a time be alone in prayer. He knew the wisdom of being in silence and solitude in order to be restored in energy and to receive inner guidance. And, here in Galilee, Jesus prepared the disciples for his leaving them:

> *I am telling you the truth: it is for your own good that I am going, because unless I go, the Paraclete will not come to you. But if I go, I will send It to you. When the Spirit of Truth comes, It will lead you to the complete truth.*

John 16:7, 13

To recall our own place of birth and growing up years, we may gain insight to soul-imprints or illusions that may continue to color the tapestry of our present lives. Yet, as Jesus explains to the disciples, we can also claim that we have the *Paraclete* to lead us to the truth. Like those of Jesus' day, we must learn to trust, to ask, to be in solitude and silence, and to receive the eternally available guidance from the Holy Spirit, who has myriad ways of blessing us with insight, comfort, forgiveness, surprises. Though it took many years to know the efficacy and joy of fully surrendering to the "still small and gentle Voice" that I've grown to trust completely, I now cannot imagine my life without this Friend.

Even with full trust in recent years, I can still be stubborn. I have often felt like a donkey being "teased" into compliance with the Spirit as Big Carrot on a stick held out in front of me and offering a new "assignment." I nibble for some time before I am ready to take the whole Carrot being offered. Even with trust, my first response more often than not is, "No way!" Yes, change is often a challenge. Yet, without exception, when I have followed the gentle proddings or big Hints of the Spirit and when I have finally reached the point where I can do no other, I have grown in ways that I could never have imagined—always with deep peace and gentle inner joy.

The enormous impact of our past experiences on our lives can become baggage we carry for a lifetime until we begin to de-create the false world we've unconsciously built. At seventy-five I still discover ego-fears to forgive from time to time; and I am now learning to forgive myself on behalf of all my sisters and brothers.[20] Again, by way of illustration of how influenced we can be from our early years, I share how Spirit can work in our daily lives with fragments of my own journey. The road to Galilee encompasses our ordinary lives, of Spirit leading us every step of the way every day, bidden or unbidden. As we Awaken, the roads seem easier to travel with journey blessings filling us with wonder, adventure, and ever-deepening love, peace, gratitude, assurance, and joy. I pray that you, dear ones, may find some insights, parallels to your own story that may act as insights to growth, or ways of using my mistakes for any learning that may be of use.

I grew up in Swampscott, Massachusetts, not far from Salem and Danvers. Like many children, I was aware of the Unseen realm that intersects with our "real" world and, as noted, I sometimes had psychic moments. What I was too young to understand was that not everyone experienced what seemed totally natural to me. My mother's fear compelled her to reprimand me. She likened me to Salem witches who were burned at the stake. She cautioned that I'd end up in the "insane asylum," as the psychiatric facility located in Danvers was then called.

For my part, I felt that because Mom seemed to be saying this was bad, I was bad; I was somehow guilty, and even had the power to cause another's death, as when I announced the impending passing of a neighbor. A self-created world of fear and illusions began to grow. Fear became a fairly constant companion, and I began to stuff down any insights or experiences from beyond the Veil, stifling potential gifts that wanted expression.

Regrettably, these ego-fears grew even deeper after the wondrous Awakening I had in Florida. What I didn't share earlier was that when the Love that had palpably embraced me for ten days departed, all the psychic energy I had repressed since childhood burst forth. The fuses often blew; the appliances no longer worked for me; I was in three places that got hit by lightning; and I began to communicate easily with folks from the Other Side. Was it any wonder that Ray began to question my sanity, which ultimately, became a crucial ingredient in our separating from our life together? Yet, the fruits of our divorce have been good for both of us and, blessedly, we remain close friends.

About twenty-five years later, when Dad was in a rehabilitation center in Las Vegas, I visited him for what I strongly sensed was to be our last visit here on earth. We sat on the edge of his bed together to chat. Much to my surprise and for the only time that I can remember, Dad took my hand in his and looking directly at me with what seemed deep concern and said, "Now Gail (my sister), you know that Nan has never been quite all right. I want you to promise me that when I'm gone, you'll take good care of her."

Since I had pretty much faced most of my ego-fear illusions— the old story I had created, and forgiven the mistakes ("sins") that had kept me separated from love by fear—I was more lovingly able to respond. "Dad," I said, "I don't want you to be embarrassed, but I'm Nan and I'm really OK. In fact, I'm able to help others now to know that they are OK, too. Gail and I will always be friends and will be there for one another. So, you don't have to worry." Dad seemed mildly embarrassed and some-what relieved, while I offered another prayer of gratitude for all the years Frank West had gently guided me through the false world of ego-fears to a free, forgiven, joy-filled, beneficial way-of-being in the world.

As you can see, I have often been a "tough nut to crack" in this journey into love and freedom. Living by my ego ways, my hopes, my dreams, making myriad mistakes, learning to trust in and surrender to the Spirit of Truth often was and sometimes continues, to be a challenge. The first time that I *consciously* answered the invitation of Spirit felt like a disaster. In the midst of prayer one day, having just offered myself to the Beloved to be ready to Serve the Spirit in *any way*, the phone rang. A woman, who had recently heard me pray aloud spontaneously during the "prayers of intercession" at church, asked if I would be the key-note speaker at the Spring Conference for Presbyterian Women in the region.

I had been far more surprised than anyone else when Some-thing or Someone within propelled me from the comfortable pew in the back to the front of the congregation: something I'd never known anyone to do during the service, least of all me. With knees shaking and in a quivering voice, yet with real authority, I shared the prayer of gratitude that welled up within me. Then I returned to the pew with utter incredulity and amazement, hav-ing acted completely out of character for who I thought myself to be!—surprised by the Spirit!

In retrospect, I believe that along with this unexpected *initia-tion* into speaking publicly, the woman and others in church that day had witnessed a promise of where the Spirit was preparing to lead me. I was *terrified* at that time to speak with more than two or three people at once. Yet, I had just offered myself in prayer, and discernment was not yet a well-developed quality within me. So, with fear and trembling, I agreed to be their keynote speaker a few months hence.

Never having spoken publicly before, I worked hard on their suggested topic, *Healing by the Spirit*, and felt reasonably prepared, material-wise, when what seemed like a day of reckoning arrived. Such is not necessarily one's best way to prepare. Fortunately for all present, the morning speaker was spirit-filled, interesting and inspiring. I will spare you the agony of my sharings; yet, can you imagine how I felt when, having spoken for a short time in a shaky voice and just beginning to relax into the sharing, a woman stood up and shouted from the rear of the auditorium, "You are grieving my spirit! Where is the crucified Christ in this talk?" It had to have been the Spirit within me that responded. I recall apologizing for making the assumption that since we were all Christian women, that everyone would know that all healing comes from the Christ Spirit, and that we are simply vessels of Christ's healing love. The rest of the day, however, is pretty much unremembered. People were polite, yet I felt I was wearing a mask of grinning steel.

When I arrived home, I wept and apologized to Whomever it was that I thought I was following. And later, much later, I gave thanks: thanks for humbling me, thanks for calling to remembrance that Jesus never wrote out his parables; he prayed and spoke from the heart, more as when I had prayed spontaneously in church. I gave thanks for helping me to walk through a deep fear of being seen and heard, of sharing my faith story. I gave thanks for helping me to see that the most important preparation for any activity is silence, solitude, and prayer. And, I gave special thanks for discovering how the Spirit can transform our weaknesses and failures by turning them into stepping stones. I even learned later that, through God's grace, several individuals gave feedback of how touched and helped they had been by my sharing. Following the Spirit is not always easy, especially during what I call the "crack me open" stages!

The next place the Spirit prodded me was to prison! I had agreed to participate with others from the church in giving the monthly birthday party in the New York State Prison for Women, a few blocks from my home. Though well-meaning, I experienced it as a ghastly affair with us "doing it for them" rather than sharing ourselves with real women who had stories to share. Ah, what a lesson to discover that what we do has far less meaning than the quality of life and the spirit that we bring to our activities. In praying forgiveness for not being authentically who I was with these women, I felt an inner injunction to offer myself as a one-to-one volunteer. (This was at the same time that I had the dream of being sent from the mountaintop to the valley below, that I shared earlier.)

The give and take with the women each week was sheer joy. Yet, my feelings as I witnessed the objectification and, often, the injustices of those incarcerated, experienced the prejudices, was exposed to the misuse of authority, and the sometimes-deplorable conditions, ranged from frustration to an old sense of powerlessness, and, ultimately, to forgiveness. Fear permeated the prison. My own spirit was sorely tested. Though I searched inwardly to find answers, a way to *really* make a change, the weekly visits seemed quite enough to me; I thought I was offering all that I could give while raising five children pretty much alone. So, I was disconcerted one November afternoon in prayer to hear, "You are to invite *all* the women at the prison to a New Year's Eve healing service." NO WAY! was my emphatic, final inner response.

Then, a whole picture began to emerge in prayer: Rev Ev, as she was called (the Reverend Evelyn Carter, whose seminars on healing and the Holy Spirit had profoundly moved me over several years) was to offer the service. I simply had to write *individual* invitations to each woman in prison; the only other "outside" individual meant to be included would be my pastor, Reverend Bruce White. Once I got the whole picture, I was relieved: first, Rev Ev would never be available; second, the prison would never give permission; and, third, my family and Bruce's family would never free us on New Year's Eve. All I had to do was contact Rev Ev and have her say, "Impossible," and I would be off the hook. So I thought!

Not wasting any time, I called around, got Rev Ev's telephone number and dialed her in Philadelphia. Since she was always on the road, I was surprised to have her answer the phone. When I made "my" request, she chuckled, "That's the Spirit for you! I'm just in the house for five minutes to change suitcases. And, I've just learned my plans for New Year's Eve have been canceled. I'd love to come!" Since Rev Ev lived by the Spirit and the Word of God, authentically "walking her talk," I've always had the feeling that she had already been clued in ahead of my call and wasn't in the least surprised.

As is the way of the Spirit, step by step, everything fell into place: permission was given, security measures taken, invitations sent out. Rev Ev arrived notwithstanding a snowstorm, the hall was packed, Bruce and I were there, and the healing service was exceptional, pure grace. What did *not* happen were all the extras that my ego-self tried to impose on the program, which I realized afterwards, would not have been appropriate to the spirit of the evening. The ego is ever vigilant to step in, blow us up with inflated self-images that keep us bound in fear. Our attitude, our thoughts, and choices make all the difference. Jesus often told his disciples to "stay awake." I'm sure such an injunction can be said much more emphatically to each one of us today.

Once again, I had learned how the Spirit wants to lead us into our own potential, this time more gently, perhaps because I was a bit more pliable and discerning. What is more, each time I followed, I grew in compassion and became less fearful. And the less fear I lived with, like an equation, the greater was my love capacity. For, "All who are guided by the Spirit of God are sons and daughters of God; for what you received was not the spirit of slavery to bring you back into fear; you received the spirit of adoption, enabling you to cry out, 'Abba!' " (Romans 8:14).

Jesus asked Peter three times, "Do you love me?" And each time Peter affirmed his love, Jesus said, "Feed my sheep." All well and good *until*, Jesus goes on: "In all truth I tell you, when you were young you put on your own belt and walked where you liked; but when you are mature you will stretch out your hands and somebody else will put a belt around you and take you where you would rather not go. Follow me" (John 21:15–19).

Imagine for a moment that Jesus is in front of you. Looking you in the eye, he asks, "Do you love me, (your name)?" How do you answer? Hear the question again, "Do you love me, (your name)?" Is your answer the same? And a third time, "Do you love me, (your name)?" What do you feel when your responses seem to be ignored? Do you choke as I have done at times when I've tried to affirm, "You know I love You." And Jesus says, "Then feed my sheep." And, what are we expected to feed them? Ourselves.

A weekend retreat with Father Henri Nouwen focusing simply on this text from John was one of those life-changing moments in my life. Inwardly, I knew without a doubt that I would be led somewhere that I would rather not go. At that time, I was looking forward to building a small hermitage on a piece of property in the woods that I had purchased in the beautiful Berkshire Mountains in Monterey, Massachusetts. When a friend saw an ad for a house with an attached liquor store for sale on the main street, he—and I sensed the Spirit agreed—insisted that I at least look at the property as a possible bookstore. Once again, no way! But I did look and though outwardly I said, "No!" inwardly, I knew that I was being asked to buy it. In an effort to "get out of it," however, I put in a ridiculously low offer, yet compromised when the owner all but accepted it. All the way to complete the sale at the bank, I kept hearing the gentle Voice within, "You will lose your money, but it will be worth it."—not too promising a beginning!

Another book could be written on how through prayer and meditation the New Spirit bookstore, which focused on spirituality, nutrition, and healthy lifestyles, quality tapes, local crafts, third world products and pieces of art, was birthed; of how it became the networking, meeting place for the local church and seven spiritual-teaching centers in the area. And, just as I was really beginning to accept that I was not to live in the woods as a "hermitess," just as I was feeling comfortable and fulfilled, the Spirit had more to teach me.

This time, I was being invited to leave the beautiful mountains, successful store and ministry, as well as the many deep and dear friendships that had grown, to live in community in an urban parish in Detroit, right where the riots had started twenty years earlier. As much as I loved Monterey, the people, and the work, a yearning had been growing within me to live in solidarity with the poor. So when the invitation came, I was easily persuaded. "Be guided by the Spirit and you will no longer yield to self-indulgence. The fruits of the Spirit are love, joy, peace, patience, kindness, goodness, trustfulness, gentleness and self control. Since we are living by the Spirit, let our behavior be guided by the Spirit" (Galations 5:16–26). These were some of the "lessons" that I was to learn in Detroit, plus a few that were more challenging.

The four years at St. Agnes were a dream come true. Hard work, long hours, no pay do not seem like heaven. Yet, I soon learned that though many may be financially challenged, more often than not, I experienced "Blessed are the poor in spirit," deeply lived out at St. Agnes parish as Love and Faith humbly in action; and as much as I offered, *always* I received far, far more. The Spirit stretched me, molded me, and granted me stronger faith, deeper appreciation of the contemplative life in the midst of city living, and a more compassionate heart. One of the special gifts of living there was to be a part of the contemplative community of about forty individuals that Father Ed developed.

One Sunday, after our monthly gathering of sitting in silence with open hearts praying over the city, country, world, and earth, one of the friends came to Father Ed and asked if there was someone who could take notes at the next gathering as she couldn't be there. Father Ed looked at me and said, "Nan can do that." Well, it didn't take long for me to ponder that taking notes on almost two hours of silence didn't make sense. So I decided to write a little newsletter of quotations that could be used as meditation starters or simply to read for inspiration. Thus was born the *Friends of Silence*[21] monthly newsletter, that has grown from the original forty to over 6,200 individual in the United States and additionally to well over one-hundred people overseas. How wondrously the Spirit will stretch us, nurture our potential, and open the door to new horizons, vaster vistas.

Another crucial learning for me in aspiring to follow the leadings of Spirit is to trust that when one door closes, something new, and more appropriate to growth, will come to birth. Just as

I thought that I was ready to commit myself permanently as a pastoral volunteer in Detroit, St. Agnes, along with thirty other churches were slated to close within six months. Previous to this, I had passed papers selling the Monterey bookstore and house, so to return to the Berkshires was no longer a viable option. My life was an open book. Though I had been looking for a small, affordable retreat house near a body of water for months, the prospects looked bleak. So, I began to move into an apartment in the city.

One day, a month before we had to vacate the rectory, Sister Mary Frances showed me an ad for a cottage with twenty-four-plus acres about two hours north of Detroit. Though I could not really afford it—predicted, I had lost much of my investment through the New Spirit ministry—we decided we needed and deserved a day off. I made an appointment to see the house the next day.

That night I had a dream of a pond with an enormous tree near it. I kept walking around the tree trying to figure out what kind of tree it was, and asking in the dream, "Who are you?" I had never seen a tree like it. As we turned into the driveway of the property for sale, I gasped. There was the pond; there was the cottonwood tree of my dream. And, we could see Lake Huron a mile down the street, the large body of water I had been looking for. Once again, I *knew* that this was to be my new home and told my friend so. Mary Fran suggested that it might be a good idea to look it over before making such a big decision.

All the while we walked the paths, through the meadow filled with wildflowers, stood in silence in the "pine cathedral," were surprised by the grotto, I kept asking myself, "Is this his bottom-line price?" I had a strong inner sense that *this is it!* When we completed the tour, had looked at the cottage, and were standing together in the kitchen, the owner asked, "What do you think?" Since I really could not afford it, I closed my eyes and repeated the thought I'd had since we arrived, "Do I have the nerve to ask him what his bottom-line price is?" As I opened my eyes, he said, "my bottom-line price is ($10,000 less than his asking price).

Take it or leave it." Without a moment's hesitation I said, "I'll take it."

How much better the Spirit knows us than we know ourselves! I sorely needed a time of tranquility, of living in solitude and silence, of re-connecting to nature, of healing the grief I was still feeling from all the church closings, a gift that I would not have accepted for myself unless prodded by the Spirit. How lavishly we are loved! Yet, without the wilderness, Jericho, Jerusalem, and Emmaus roads, I wonder how ready I would have been for urban, community life, and then, for a time of being alone in the woods with the Alone.

I continued to discover how readily and creatively our prayers can be answered by the Spirit, how we are all One with All. My first Spring season on the land when I was walking through the woods the day before Pentecost, I noted the small bridge over the creek had been broken by snowmobiles that had come down from an open meadow whipping through the paths leading to the grotto and pond. Their noise, pollution, and destruction had frustrated me all winter. I studied the opening to the big field where they originated and tried to figure out a friendly, safe solution to keeping snowmobiles out, but to no avail. Giving up, I threw my arms up in a gesture of supplication and simply called out, "Help, please!"

The winds were strong all Pentecost Sunday. I remarked to several friends how appropriate these gusts of Wind Spirit were. The next day, my friend Patricia, who often visited from Detroit, and I went for a walk through the woods. When we came to what used to be the opening onto the field, *nada*. The opening was gone. A huge, maple tree, felled by the Pentecost winds, now covered the opening to the path so naturally, one would think it had always been there. Yet, for the remaining years that I was there, the tree's branches continued to grow leaves, transform its dress into colorful array in the fall, and then bare itself for winter sleep. What an answer to prayer.

Nature can be a strong reminder of the beauty, unity, and harmony of Creation, as well as a terrible and devastating power that, it seems to me, is meant to awaken. Nature is universal and seems to call us to Awaken to the Oneness we all are, inter-being with one another and with Creation itself. I experienced this first in my own awakening in Florida; then, in so many times and ways during my sojourn in the woods, as in the following surprising event.

Patricia, her collie, and I were walking slowly and quietly through the woods seeking out the old fallen tree that a raccoon family called home. As we meandered along, I asked her if she knew where all the winter birds that came to the feeders in the winter spent their time in the summer. She didn't know. When we came to the raccoon's resting place, they were not at home, so we offered our greetings to their unseen presence and continued on to a moss-covered mound, which we called our fairy ring, between two trees, and sat down to rest. Even Timmy, her dog, seemed to bask in the Silence.

After perhaps ten minutes or so, we noticed tiny birds were flying into the branches all around us and breaking out into song. Twenty-five-to-thirty-or-so chickadees, nuthatches, finches, and several wee birds unknown to us flitted from branch to branch coming closer and closer: a symphony of birdsong. We were gifted with one of those timeless moments, of perhaps three-to-five minutes, where you hold your breath lest you discover 'tis but a dream. But this was real, pure grace, and an answer to my question. Then, just as suddenly as they had appeared, they disappeared back again silently into the woods. Our only response was silent wonder, a welling up of tears, and deep gratitude.

Though I had heard inwardly the gentle, guiding Voice of Love informing me that my time in the woods would be for three years, I ignored It. After all, ego assured me that I was a good steward of the land, sharing it with folks from Detroit eighty miles away whenever they felt the need for silence, solitude, and rest, I counseled a few individuals, and, in general, I led a life of prayer in communion with Nature. Ego illusions were deafening me to the trusted Voice I aspired *always to* follow. We must be ever-vigilant to the wily ways of the tempter.

Having procrastinated with no initiative to move on, another sign was given to me. I was visited by one of Nature's unheralded creatures on a rare hot and humid night in my heavenly haven. I had gone to bed early, dozing fitfully for hours. Around one o'clock I heard scratching in the woodburning stove. Assuming a bird had flown down the flue, I switched on the light over the bed and got up to look. What a surprise to discover a rather larger-than-usual brown bat hovering in the corner. I told sister bat that I'd take care of her in the morning, closed the stove door, and returned to bed. Within minutes I heard what sounded to me as loud as a sea gull flying around the room. Deciding that perhaps bat had somehow escaped, I pulled up the sheet to cover myself just in time. She landed directly over my solar plexus area. When I fanned the sheet up and down, she flew away as I announced aloud, "I'm not comfortable with this much closeness to you." I turned over and pulled the sheet over my head just as she landed again—this time on my back in what would also be the solar plexus area.

It then dawned on me: bats can't see in the light. So I reached up and turned the light back on. Knowing how interrelated we are with *all* of creation, I began to ask myself what sister bat's message might mean for me. I got up and headed for my little prayer room and library—checking at the doorway where bat was now hanging. I located *Medicine Cards*, by Jamie Sams, a book that describes the energy of various animals. Bats' energy is that of re-birth, new beginnings. It didn't take me long to discern her gift. I loved living in the woods so close to earth's myriad blessings. Yet now, I thought that I could no longer ignore what I'd heard in meditation, that it was time to move on.

Even so, more than halfway through the fourth year, my rebellion continued and turned into a life-threatening case of pneumonia-influenza. I was pretty much bedridden and stubbornly neglected to see a doctor: a stubborn stance that well could have set me back years of health if I didn't die first—talk about ego-inflation! Remember, I said we avoid following this gracious, generous, guiding Voice, which *always* has our best interest at heart, at our peril. Now, having learned so many lessons the hard way,

I can say that I am far more consciously choosing to walk my talk with integrity and faith.

Following the leadings of the Spirit on this journey into Love is far easier day by day, then when major changes are on the horizon. Yet, I have grown from being like those in Scripture who may say *no* at first, to a woman who now moves far more quickly into the flow and joy of following Spirit's wise Voice of guidance. In fact, *knowing* the loving ministrations of the Beloved, of the Holy Spirit, angels, and Inner Self as guide has become a way of life. It's a rare day that I do not say, "Thank you . . . thank you . . . thank you" for answers, for guidance. We are ever being given invitations to grow in Love and clarity of Purpose. How we respond makes all the difference.

Our resistances most often indicate the presence of fear. While I had no fear of sister bat, what I did fear was leaving what had become for me "heaven on earth." I had become attached to living alone with days of silence and living prayer, communing with all of nature's wonders, the proximity to water, just Be-ing.

After recognizing and accepting what I needed to do, I prayed the prayer of abandonment, asked forgiveness for my ego-filled arrogance, and called a realtor to give an estimate as I prepared to sell "my" heavenly haven and hermitage. Not surprisingly, three days later I was healed and fully restored, now that I'd answered the "invitation" to yet a new life, a new adventure. And, no surprise, it has once again turned out to bring more joy, love, new friendships, and lived purpose than I'd ever imagined it could.

I left for the East Coast to visit family and, while there, was invited to live in the studio apartment over the garage with my son, Mark, and the family's home in Vermont. This time, the Spirit had "driven" me (since I was reluctant to go on my own) to where I was most able to extend love—our purpose for this sojourn on Earth. Susan, Mark's wife, had developed Chronic Fatigue Syndrome, the debilitating environmentally induced disease thought to be brought on by exposure to chemicals, pollution, and other bi-products of our wounded earth home. My grandchildren, Samantha and Austin, were still quite young when

I moved in. How right it was to be able to fill in as Nana Nan with the children, while offering a helping hand to Susan and Mark for many years as Susan slowly regained her health and strength. I was inspired by the tower of stability that Mark was through it all, and by Susan, who saved all her energy to be a real Mom presence to the children whenever they were around. I learned anew how love *is* strength and trust in action. Still, my true Home will ever be in the Heart of Love, where we know our Oneness with All in the Peace of God.

By the millennium, Friends of Silence had grown to the point where it was more and more difficult to send the newsletter out by myself. Anne Strader and Barbara Taylor had both been long-time friends of Silence, and felt a commitment to become a part of its ministry. So, the three of us began to pray and to look for just the right place to establish a permanent center. Though I expected it to be founded in Vermont, The Friends of Silence Peace and Prayer Center became a reality in Hannibal, Missouri. Since I was already living in Vermont, it became clear that I would divide my time between the Hannibal Center and Jericho branch. I had determined that I could *never* live in Hannibal during the hot and humid summer months. You'd think by now I would have learned not to say, "never."

Within two weeks of my wintertime in Hannibal, I was diagnosed with stage-4 cancer, had an operation, and ended up with six months of chemo treatments, pneumonia, and two embolisms to my lung . . . seven months including the entire summer. Yet, what a *blessing* filled with so many lessons and insights it turned out to be! We all soon recognized with gratitude, how providential, how right Hannibal is for the Center in the heartland of the nation, and how amazingly well the three of us work as colleagues and friends in following the Spirit.

What a perfect place it turned out to be for my healing. I made a conscious choice to ask and allow the Spirit, guides, and angels to guide me through this *experience* of cancer for as long as it was needed. From the diagnosis to the healing, I literally felt *no* fear. Once again, I was aware of the freedom of not being in fear's grip. I chose to live this as simply an experience of cancer and chemo processing through my physical body. It helped to *know* that I am not my body; rather, like all of us, I am spirit dwelling for a time in a physical "house." I am already whole in spirit, and I trusted wholeness was manifesting in my body day by day. I was not an ideal patient, refusing to hear any explanations, prognoses, or possible side-effects. I refused to say or to let anyone around me say that I *had* cancer. That felt too much like owning it; I did not want to give cancer any power with words or thoughts.

I was blessed beyond belief by every doctor who cared for me; the facilities and all the staff from nurses to food servers, from technicians to the social workers and volunteers, *everyone* I met or was with seemed to be at one with their particular part of the healing ministry, *everything* was gift. I felt so embraced by the many new friends who found ways to make the process easier, I often forgot that I needed to take it easy. Anne and Barb graciously became my major support team at home; friends jumped in to help almost daily. My children, grandchildren, sister, Ray, and so many friends from near and far kept in touch in too many ways to innumerate.

Prayer was the foundation of my life all those months. Prayers came in by mail, the Internet, calls, and visits. The day before the surgery, about a dozen individuals came for an hour of silence sitting in a circle. At the closing, Father Mike invited everyone to come lay hands on me offering healing prayer. Angels seemed to be among us in the room. The silence felt full of peace. When I asked in prayer for a word to carry with me, "I heard," the lesson here is to learn to *receive*," an ever-growing edge in my life. Yet, what a joy! This became a balance to being a workaholic for much of my life and seemed to help me feel in harmony with All during those months that led to healing. And I certainly grew in understanding the power of prayer and the blessings of a community responding with love.

I live in expectation, always with an intention to be open to the next leading by the Spirit. O, to live the Mystery! Some days are wilderness days; some days I travel the Jericho road to be with a neighbor. Praying over the world brings many Jerusalem moments and, more and more, I experience Emmaus moments, many of them during the months of healing in Hannibal. Each day I sense the invitation to celebrate the Divine Source, even knowing that somewhere down the road, I can easily be asked to travel another road I would rather not take. I may say, "No way!" And then, most likely, I will go with joy in my heart.

The Spirit is always sending us out to bring the Good News, the gifts of God, and our unique gifts to one another and to receive with gratitude the gifts of God from others who offer their gifts of love, as well. Reciprocity and mutuality maintain the balance. As the world grows closer, we are called to give birth to a new earth, a new global community, a new City of Love where all can pray and dialogue in peace, a New Dawn. This will happen inasmuch as each individual chooses to move out of his or her own fear-filled world within and become a dwelling place of healing Love. To believe in love, peace, and all the qualities that Jesus exemplified is not enough; in fact, simply to believe can be dangerous. Until we apply these essential characteristics within ourselves, we consciously or unconsciously project our fear-illusions out to others, to groups of people, and can easily feel smug with our good intentions.

To follow the roads that are the way of the Beloved which lead to the peace beyond our usual way of understanding, is to become vulnerable, to discover those areas in our lives that are in need of forgiveness and reconciliation, to live with heartfelt gratitude, compassion, and assurance. The foundation must ever be prayer with times to pause and be still, to spend some time in solitude and silence. To awaken to the journey is to offer our Selves as co-creators, co-lovers, and co-workers with the living Christ, who dwells within every open heart. In following, we soon realize 'tis all but a prelude to living with deep, abiding peace and gentle joy.

A new earth is arising, a heightened consciousness is emerging, where beauty, harmony, sharing, right action, and joy will embrace the planet. All who Awaken to the energy of LoveConsciousness will become gateways to extend Love and Light into the world. And as more and more, millions and millions,

Awaken, our home planet will begin to know its own sacredness. Listen deeply in the silence and there you will be blessed with peace and love at the sacred altar within your own soul.

"Through Love's Spirit may you grow firm in the power with regard to your Inner Self, so that Christ may live in your hearts through faith; and then, planted in love and built on love, with all of the Beloved's holy people you will have the strength to grasp the breadth and length, and height and depth; so that, knowing the love of Christ, which is beyond knowledge, you may be filled with the utter fullness of Love (Ephesians 3:16–19).

May Love bless you, one and all!

Nan

Notes

1. I first heard the phrase, *yesterday's will of God*, in a fourteen week training course given by Walter Wink, a New Testament theologian and scholar. As we recognize that creation continues each day and, in time, replaces outmoded habits and thought patterns, we experience a vibrant, loving energy that blesses ourselves and the world. Hearts and minds open to new ways-of-being informed by authentic old values can give way to new, more life-giving models for individuals as well as most institutions including religious organizations. Without Walter Wink's insights and ground-breaking work, *Using the Bible for Human Transformation*, this book never would have been possible. I am greatly indebted and grateful to Walter and June Wink for their friendship, support, and their lives, which give witness to and serve in the Awakening thrust and power of Love in action.

2. I choose to use the combined words *LoveConsciousness* to refer to the Word and often to God. LoveConsciousness denotes a combining of feminine and masculine qualities, a melding of heart and mind energies, that helps to clarify my understanding. *Logos* is a masculine word that seems to point to an imbalance, a mind without a heart. Please, I encourage anyone who doesn't resonate with this Name to retain or to choose words or phrases that are more resonant with your own heart and mind throughout this, our journey into Love.

3. I find the word *kindom* far more descriptive and balanced than *kingdom*, a masculine word implying a role Jesus refused to embrace during his time of temptation and discernment in the wilderness.

4. In the early 1970s I entered into eight years of counseling with Frank E. West, whom I always found to be a sensitive and clear channel of Love. Much of each session was based on the question, "What are you afraid of?" no matter what issue I presented. At

first, my fears were like a sticky ball of spaghetti, a myriad mess; yet, little by little, I regained more and more of my true essence. My life was inexorably enhanced, changed, and blessed beyond belief from facing those pain-filled, neurotic, obsessive, awakening in consciousness years. Without Frank's patient guidance, I can't even imagine what my life might have been. Everything I have been able to create and offer in Service is colored by his care-filled walking with me. And the ripple effect with my children, grandchildren, with individuals that I have counseled, as well as my friendships is a gift that continues to multiply. My gratitude for this man of integrity and wisdom is unending. And I hope, in as much as I am able, to radiate the peace, love, and sense of well-being that he extends out to others in the world.

5. *The Dean's Watch* by Elizabeth Goudge, renewed in 1988 by C.S. Gerard Kealey and Jessie Munroe, published by Servant Publications, P. O. Box 8617, Ann Arbor, Michigan 48107. Used with permission.

6. *A Wind in the Door* by Madeleine L'Engle, Farrar, Straus, & Giroux.

7. Lucifer's name comes from the Latin words, *lux*, meaning light and *feare*, meaning "to bear" . . . thus, the light-bearer. As Jesus meets the tempter in the wilderness, he is en*light*ened and able to discern his mission and purpose. When we face temptation, Lucifer may be inviting us to say "no" to yesterday's will of God and/or to discover, choose, and claim our own truth in relation to purpose.

8. The Very Reverend Alan Jones, Dean, Grace Cathedral in San Francisco, CA. Quoted from "Grace Notes," January 1992; used with permission, April 8, 1993.

9. Nicolas Roerich: artist, author, philosopher, educator, peacemaker. The Roerich Peace Pact is a remarkable treaty that sought to preserve cultural monuments during times of war. It was signed by President Roosevelt and other world leaders earning Roerich a nomination for the Nobel Peace Prize. You can find further information as well as enjoy some of his original paintings at the Roerich Museum on West 107th Street in New York City.

10. *Flute Solo,* can be found in *My Song Is of Mercy* by Fr. Matthew Kelty and is used with the kind permission of the author.

11. Thomas Hora, M.D., a God-centered, spiritual seeker and psychiatrist, founded the N. Y. Institute of Metapsychiatry, authored many books and booklets including *Beyond the Dream, Dialogues*

in Metapsychiatry, and *One Mind,* edited by Susan von Reichenbach, the latest legacy of his spiritual teachings.

12. One Mind refers to the one true Mind in which we all move and have our being.

13. *A Course in Miracles* is a one year Course that can be taken by anyone seeking to find their own Internal Teacher. The book consists of a Text, a Workbook of daily exercises, and a Manual for Teachers. The course helps the student distinguish between the real and unreal, between knowledge and perception. The aim of the Course is to remove the obstacles to the awareness of Love's presence, our natural birthright.

14. *Powers and Principalities* is a most timely Trilogy by Walter Wink and includes: 1. *Naming the Powers,* 2. *Unmasking the Powers,* and 3. *Engaging the Powers.*

15. Judas: I just want to acknowledge that new discoveries, including *The Gospel of Judas,* are opening up new questions as to his role in the Crucifixion of Jesus. At the very least, we can be open to any new light shining into the corridors of history and ponder any new insights from reasonably reliable information.

16. "An inconvenient truth." The book and/or the video *An Inconvenient Truth,* by Al Gore, are a must for all in order to spread the seeds of peace and healing for the planet Earth: our One home. I truly believe that our choosing to be willing to change our ways of living on this planet, individually and globally, so that future generations will inherit a viable planet to live on must be the first priority of every individual and nation, no matter how real the inconveniences may seem.

17. The Guild for Spiritual Guidance is a two-year apprentice program that seeks to develop a heightened awareness of the many and diverse ways God is present in and to the world. For further information, write to: Sally C. Woodhall, Director, 68 Harrison Lane, Bethlehem, CT 06751.

18. Sr. Meg: Sr. Margaret Funk, is a retreat leader, Director of the School of *Lectio Divina,* Beech Grove, IN, and the author of several books including *Thoughts Matter, Tools Matter, Humility Matters.*

19. *Peace Planet: Light for the World* by Nan Merrill and Barbara Taylor is published by Friends of Silence and can be purchased for $15 at: *FOS Peace and Prayer Gifts,* c/o Barbara Taylor, 200 Rock Street, Hannibal, MO 63401.

20. Forgiveness: In *A Course in Miracles*, to forgive is to heal. As we forgive our brothers and sisters, we restore to truth what was denied by both individuals. "We will see forgiveness where we have given it."

21. *Friends of Silence* is a non-profit endeavor to facilitate others in reverencing silence, prayer, contemplation, the Divine Guest, and the Oneness of all creation as well as to encourage the life-giving empowerment that derives from the Silence. For further information or to be added to the mailing list, write to:

Friends of Silence: Center for Peace and Prayer
c/o Anne L. Strader
11 Cardiff Lane
Hannibal, MO 63401

PART 2

Love Song of the New Dawn

A Soul Journey
Illustrations by Phoebe Darlington

Preface

Love Song of the New Dawn was birthed unexpectedly during two meditations while I was visiting my friend, Elaine, in Santa Fe. She had called when I was living alone in the Michigan woods and all but insisted that I come help "break" her writer's block; "I was to force her," if necessary, to complete her Jungian thesis, which was nearing a last deadline; and which she was able to do—just barely.

On two occasions when Elaine left to spend the evening with friends, I chose to remain at home in silence and solitude. The first evening when I was in deep silence, this story seemed to present itself. I simply jotted notes creating an outline even as I remained in the "presence" of the Silence. The next evening, the bones of the outline were fleshed out following a long meditation. With the exception of one or two words, *Love Song* remains as I wrote it then.

In 1994, I had fifty spiral copies printed for family and friends; many called to share how helpful it had been for their own soul's journey. Then, in the midst of rewriting *Journey into Love*, I realized that *Love Song* holds the golden gifts that we integrate into our lives as our fears are diminished and, finally, released. In retrospect, I also realized that Dancing Star of my long ago dream that I shared as the basement dream on pages (93–96), has been fully integrated into my psyche through the writing of this book, as if we were somehow co-authors.

I pray that Dawn Bringer of this story will walk into your life in one way or another, dear friends, to bestow the blessings that will be most life-giving for you. Walk in Beauty; walk in Peace . . . Be love. Be loved.

Just after midnight on the eve of the Spring Equinox, Dancing Star awakened suddenly from the Dreamtime. She gasped. For, standing silently by her bedside was a shining being who radiated beams of love.

"Come with me, my child, if you will," she said, extending her graceful hands toward Dancing Star, who cautiously accepted the invitation. In what seemed only a heartbeat, they were deep in a forest.

Dancing Star shivered and asked in a quivering voice, "Who are you? What do you want with me?"

"I am Dawn Bringer. I am a friend to all who are ready to awaken to new life. Now, I have three questions to put to you before I tell you my reason for bringing you here. First, do you trust me?"

"I think so," Dancing Star surprised herself by answering so quickly.

"Do you trust yourself?"

"Oh, I've been painfully learning to trust myself for ever so long. I think I do now."

"A special journey awaits you, if you feel ready. I will be with you in spirit, but you must enter the underworld alone. Seven doors will be opened to you, if you choose to travel down the stairs. Should you want to return at any time, you can call my name and I'll be there. Do you feel ready to walk this path?"

"Yes, Dawn Bringer. It feels right in my heart and my head seems to agree. Can you show me the road I am to travel?

"It's right before us, my child, though hidden by old leaves from last fall's tree sheddings." Then Dawn Bringer walked over near a tall sturdy oak tree, brushed aside the moldering mass of earth compost, which revealed an old wooden trap door.

Dancing Star was startled. "You don't expect me to climb through there, I hope!"

"I will give you directions just once, so listen carefully," answered Dawn Bringer. "After that, you are free to go on the journey or to return home. If you choose to open the door to the underworld, you will find a long set of stairs. You are to go down seven, times seven. At the bottom of each set of seven stairs will be a door. You are to knock on each door in turn and meet a man who will have a gift for you. After you have received his gift, ask to meet his companion. Then, as you are ready, excuse yourself and travel seven stairs to the next door. Be sure to note how things look along the way. If you are ready, I shall leave you alone now, though know my spirit is ever with you. If you wish to return home, take my hand and I will lead you. Blessings be with you, my child."

Dancing Star stood still. Not a sound could
be heard in the forest: no rustling leaves, no birdsong,
no animals scurrying. She could feel her heart
pounding and knew that if she did not move soon,
fears would rise up and doubts would distract her
from the path. So taking a deep breath, she tugged on the
latch-ring and raised the trap door.

As she started down the first seven stairs,
she felt as if she were entering a womb cave. The
earthy odor reminded her of the refreshing fragrance
of a summer rain after a long drought. Not one to take
nature for granted, Dancing Star felt right at home.
As she took the seventh step, she saw a beautifully
polished oak door with roses carved like a bower
around the frame. The brass knob had been corroded
by time and dampness. She hesitated and then knocked
timidly on the door. To her surprise, a small, wizened old
man slowly opened the door. He looked like the Druids
she loved so much in her books of fairy tales.

"Well now," he said, "if it isn't a joy to meet you! Come in, come in and be welcome, my dear child! I'm called Elbert."

"Thank you," responded Dancing Star, who did indeed feel the welcome. "I'm pleased to meet you."

"And I'm supposing you'll be wanting the gift I've held for you for many a year? Yes?"

"Yes, if you please. I was told you'd have a gift for me."

"Well now, 'tis right here, it is." And Elbert handed her a beautifully bound book.

When Dancing Star opened it to read the title, however, she found only blank pages. She felt a little disappointed.

Before she could question Elbert, his wife entered the room. "I, too, am so happy to meet you, Dancing Star. I am Princess Selene."

Dancing Star smiled. Never in her life had she seen a being who looked so young, yet so old, at the same time—ageless beauty. "Oh," was the most she could utter.

Princess Selene returned her smile. "Before you continue on your journey, my dear one, I want you to write your name on the first page of this book, for it is to be the love song of your new life, the new dawn." And she handed Dancing Star a luminous pen.

Having carefully written her name in the book, Dancing Star felt it was time to depart. "I must go on," she said, "but I do so hope to meet you both again some day. Thank you for your gifts to me." And she left as she had come through the oak door on the seventh stair.

On the very next step, the scenery suddenly changed. The sweet fragrance of pine trees blended with birdsong, though she saw no birds. Pine needles graced the steps, soft and slightly slippery under her feet. When she reached the fourteenth stair, Dancing Star found the door half-hidden by a tree of life that was inscrolled on the door and all around it. She admired the lovely crafted artwork before knocking loudly three times with the metal knocker, which was shaped like a pine cone.

She was astounded when the door was opened by an enormous bearded man, a giant, whose demeanor exuded gentleness and tenderness. "So glad to have the pleasure of your acquaintance, my dear. My name is Yves."

"Hello. I'm Dancing Star."

"Oh, I know your name . . . I know you very well. I'm here to help you on the way."

"Thank you, Yves. You are kind," said Dancing Star feeling it would be rude to ask if he had a gift for her.

As if reading her heart's concern, Yves said, "Oh yes, my dear, I do have a gift for you to take into the new dawn. Let me get it for you." He reached into a hollowed niche too high for Dancing Star to see and brought forth a canvas bag with a shoulder strap. He asked her to reach inside for her gift.

When Dancing Star put her hand down to the bottom of the bag, she felt a cold piece of metal that turned out to be a silver lock and key. Looking at it carefully, she saw her name engraved in exquisite calligraphy along with decorative stars. "How beautiful," she exclaimed.

"This little token is to remind you to call upon me if you should ever need outer strength or protection. I will always be nearby, my dear. And now, I will call my companion. First though, I must warn you not to be afraid." Yves then let out a throat sound, too eerie to describe.

Before Dancing Star had time to wonder why she might be afraid, a sleek lynx came bounding into the room from an entrance she had not noticed. "I call her Lilith," Yves said. "Come, stand beside her so that your energies can meld. Lilith shares my gift to you. She will be the protector of your inner hidden life. You can call upon her at any time to protect you from negative thought forms.

Dancing Star stared into Lilith's eyes. They communicated such a deep level of trust and understanding that she soon came close enough to stroke her lustrous coat. Though she would have enjoyed lingering there, Dancing Star felt compelled to be on her way. "How can I ever thank you? I'm so glad to know I can always call upon you for help. But for now, I must go." Placing her lock and key and her precious book in the canvas bag, she gave her two new friends a hug and left them standing side-by-side in the doorway.

By the time Dancing Star reached the next step, the scene changed abruptly. She felt enveloped by a deep forest. Roots and thickets grew into the stairs making her progress so slow that to traverse the remaining steps seemed to take hours. Finally, she reached the twenty-first stair. Pulling aside a big leafy branch, she discovered a rickety swinging door with no lock or knob. As she wondered how to make her presence known, the door swung open. A young American wearing a simple and plain loincloth with a bag around his neck stood before her. "I am Spotted Owl," he said in a voice that conveyed assurance, and he motioned her to enter.

Dancing Star's heart beat faster. Spotted Owl was handsome and she felt an immediate attraction. Then, she started to speak, "I guess you know that I am on a very special journey." She hesitated. All the words she wanted to utter became jumbled in her mind. So she closed her eyes, took a deep breath, and found her Center once again. When she opened her eyes, Spotted Owl was smiling at her with a look of compassionate amusement.

"Yes, I know you well and I wish you well." Then he took the white-skin medicine bag decorated with colorful beads from his neck and placed it around Dancing Star's neck. The bag lay directly over her heart. "Later, when you are ready," he said, "you will find two stones in the medicine bag: a 'magic' stone from a distant star that will aid you in discerning the truth, and a turquoise gem to help you speak and act with wisdom."

Dancing Star remained speechless. She was filled with gratitude and love, sensing how crucial discernment and wisdom would be in order to live with integrity. Before she could voice her deep-felt feelings, Spotted Owl invited his wife to join them.

Without introduction, she addressed Dancing Star, who was further overcome by the simplicity and beauty she radiated. "I am Turtledove," she said. "In my name is a gift to carry in your heart: the turtle will ground your energy in dove's peace. For only those with peace-filled ways grounded in heart-love will be able to be builders of the new dawn. Go now and walk in Beauty. Share our gifts to you with all you meet along life's path."

Dancing Star's silence and tears were all the thanks she could render, as she carried the image of Spotted Owl and Turtledove's arms raised in blessing to the next seven stairs on her journey.

Now the forest turned to walls of huge stone, standing like monoliths on either side of the stairway path, which was made of solid, steel-blue rock. Dancing Star felt cold and shivered as she walked slowly down to the twenty-eighth step. No door was visible, but she noted a large, round rock covering what looked to be the entrance to a cave. A lead pipe hung from a nail-like projection over the rock. She took the pipe and hit the rock creating an echo that reverberated throughout the stairwell. Without warning, the rock rolled to one side.

Dancing Star peered into the dark dwelling.
As her eyes adjusted to the shadows, she could see
the form of a man covered with skins—a caveman!
Not knowing how to address such a one, she wondered
how they could ever have a meaningful conversation.
As she looked into his eyes, she heard a voice deep
within her, "I am Egore." She jumped back and
scratched her head in puzzlement.

Then Egore, with a few guttural sounds, made
Dancing Star understand that she was to look once again
into his eyes. No sooner had she done so, when she
heard the inner voice say, "My gift to you is the ability
to communicate without words."

The gratitude that welled up in Dancing Star's
heart was heard more clearly by Egore than the words
Thank you so very much, which she spoke.

When Egore grunted again, she immediately gazed
into his eyes. Her heart's voice sounded again. "Meet my
friend, Riva." When Dancing Star turned to look into the
corner where he was pointing, she saw an enormous mother
bear with two cubs nestled by her side. Looking back into Egore's
eyes, she heard, "Riva offers you warmth and comfort of heart to
carry home. When you think of us, we will arise in your spirit."

Recognizing that it was time to depart, Dancing Star
made it known to Egore through her heart-thoughts that she
wished to kiss each of his eyes that had so blessed her.
As she kissed them, a deep seeing seemed to be awakened
within her. "I leave you all with thanksgiving and my love,"
she thought as she took a last look into Egore's eyes.

He nodded and voiced a final guttural sound that
felt to Dancing Star like a warm embrace.

Before going on, Dancing Star sat down on the step outside of Egore and Riva's cave home. She wondered if to receive even one more gift wouldn't be gluttonous and greedy. Withdrawing into her Center, she soon realized that not one of the gifts was for herself alone. Each one would make her way-of-being in the world more beneficial to others. And knowing that to be true, she was ready to continue.

Dancing Star now noticed that the rock walls had changed to sandstone; the steps were deep with sand, making progress slow and tedious. Reaching the thirty-fifth step, she was surprised to see an enormous tent with an opening akin to a door. Before she could peek inside to make herself known, a tall sheik dressed in many fine layers of silk came out to welcome her and lead her inside.

The interior was so palatial and so filled with myriad treasures that Dancing Star was momentarily stunned. Many beautiful women dressed in pastel-gauze garments seemed to dance to the soft, harmonious melodies that permeated the room as they worked, oblivious to the newcomer in their midst.

The sheik's loud voice startled her. "My name is Abdul Raheem. I can only offer you the gift of never again wanting for material goods. As you work to build the New Dawn, sharing your truth with others, your needs will be met." And Abdul Raheem handed her a gold piece to remind her of his gift.

"Oh, that is wonderful!" Dancing Star exclaimed. "With my needs met, I will be able to give myself totally to the great Work ahead. Thank you. May I meet your wife now?" she asked, wondering to herself about the many women who seemed to flow harmoniously as one.

Abdul Raheem beckoned Dancing Star to follow him through the long strands of gemlike beads that served as a door. She saw a slight woman whose face was partially veiled sitting as one in prayer. Sensing their presence, she opened her eyes and greeted them with a simple bowing of her head.

"Please meet Pearl, a woman grace-filled and worthy. Silence is the friend she offers you as gift. It will lead you to the true Treasure deep within your soul." Pearl looked into her eyes, nodded again and returned to her meditation. Dancing Star whispered her thanks and followed Abdul Raheem out to the main hall.

"Here, take these for refreshment on the next part of your journey," he said, handing Dancing Star a small bag of dates and a canteen of precious water. He then led her back to the stairs.

Once outside the tent, Dancing Star ate a few of the luscious, fresh dates, and drank deeply of the water in the canteen. Then, she placed them and the gold piece in her canvas bag along with the book, pen, and lock and key, and started down the stairs.

All at once, the sand gave way to a rough road of dirt and stones. She seemed to be walking down into an ancient city. As she progressed down the seven stairs, she was disconcerted to sense the spirits of those who had left the earthly plane coming and going on the stairway. Upon reaching the forty-second step, she looked as usual for the door on the right-hand side. Finding none there, she felt drawn to examine the left side. She soon came face-to-face with a cold, black onyx door. With an apprehensive shudder and great timidity, she knocked three times.

Just as she thought no one would answer, the door slowly opened. A fully dressed skeleton appeared, pointed it's bony finger to the gloomy room inside and bade Dancing Star enter. Recalling the lock and key, and Yves's promise of strength and protection, she sent him an inner call. Immediately, she felt his powerful inner strength, blended with Turtledove's grounding peace, penetrate her being. Then, she walked with confidence into the house of Death.

"Bravo, my child. Most individuals try to ignore me and the gifts I have to give. To welcome me into your life is to die to those things that inhibit your growth. To live with the uncertainty of my presence brings a keener appreciation of life to every moment. I, myself, am the gift that I offer you —the awareness that each breath, each relationship, each opportunity is precious beyond measure for growth into wholeness. Be mindful of me as you walk the earth road."

Dancing Star tried her best to take in all that Death had said, knowing it was important. Dying to the old habits, fears, relationships which hold one back takes courage and a willingness. She knew that every gift she had been given would be needed and useful, if she were to accept the gifts of Death. She also knew that in order to be truly free, she had no choice but to befriend Death.

As she smiled her unreserved assent, a shining Being entered the room filling it with light. "I am Dyanna, dear one. you have made the choice that entitles you to my gift—the Light to lead you into new Life. Remember: I will always go before you, cutting a path through any darkness along the road. Call on me as you will."

Dancing Star wanted so much to hug Dyanna before leaving, but she definitely did not feel ready to hug Death. So she simply gave them each her gratitude and blessing as she left through the door that Death held open for her.

Remaining on the stair, Dancing Star ate another date and drank a few sips of water, grateful once again for Abdul Raheem's kindness. As she stepped on the first of the last seven steps, she felt energized. The stair was made of pure crystal. She held her breath in wonder at the scene before her. Dazzling Light in the underworld? She was amazed.

Almost with reluctance, she slowly started down the steps, for she wished to savor forever the magnificent panorama that she saw before her. The last stair, the forty-ninth step, was fashioned of rose quartz, which was in keeping with the door that was now before her. Dancing Star felt tears well up as she examined the intricate designs of inlaid rose quartz in the door paneling and around the framework of exquisite, crystal-cut roses that exuded an energy and a scent of Beauty. Then she noticed a clear crystal bell, which she rang. The sound seemed to penetrate into the core of her being.

To her utter amazement, Dancing Star recognized
the man who opened the door: the One whom she had loved
for all eternity, the Heart of her heart. Overcome with joy,
she opened herself to the waves of bliss that pulsated with
indescribable musical colors. Then, Dancing Star and the
Beloved of her heart embraced becoming one whole and holy
Being of Light and Love. He led Her to the canopied bridal
bed with coverlets of pure, rose-colored silk, where they
tenderly expressed their love fully and without reserve.
He was Gift to Her; She was Gift to Him . . . and a Holy Child
was conceived, a creative Gift to the world.

Though it wrenched her heart to have to part after their time together was complete, Dancing Star knew that in the perfect timing of the Universe they would be reunited forever. As they lingered together at the door for a final embrace, her Beloved placed a golden ring on her finger with a smile that was a promise. Then, after opening the door, He of her heart pointed to yet another set of stairs. He told her to open the trap door to the world when she came to the bottom and to remember all that she would see.

After a final touch of their fingertips, Dancing Star looked ahead as she started to descend the steps. But, it took every gift that she had received not to be afraid; for she now seemed to be in the ethereal atmosphere of an abyss —nothingness. Still, her feet seemed to be on solid ground. When she reached the seventh step, there was indeed a trap door, though it, too, seemed to be made out of emptiness except for a jewel-studded ring.

She trembled as she pulled the door up; and she gasped when she saw Mother Earth spinning before her. Angels and the spirits of loving souls encircled the planet like a Great Spinning Cross. Dancing Star could see that they were mending Mother Earth's web that had been broken in many, many places. She could see innumerable groups of individuals on Her skin, who were helping the populace harmonize with the vibrations of the Compassionate One now radiating in every heart. She saw that the souls of those who were unable to withstand the Beams of Love were being lifted up by Light-beamed satellites, which would take them to stars of compatible vibration so that they could continue awakening to Love and Light.

As she continued to marvel at the vision before her, Dancing Star's Heart Voice told her to shut the trap door and to close her eyes. For the briefest moment, she entered the Eternal Now: past, present, and future as One. She was all time and space with all other beings. Then, when she opened her eyes, she was kneeling at her bedside as in prayer. Sunrays were just beginning to radiate a new day as she looked out of the window.

She stood up. Had this journey been but a dream, she wondered? Then she saw her Beloved's golden ring on her finger and felt the canvas bag with its gifts still on her shoulder.

Suddenly, Dawn Bringer was standing beside her. "You have walked the path with love and integrity, my friend. You have seen the Work needed to heal the Mother. Do you feel ready to abandon yourself in Service to the Great Plan?"

Dancing Star did not hesitate. "Yes, I desire nothing more."

"Welcome then, my child," she said. "You, too, are now a bringer of the New Dawn. Go in peace to radiate the Love . . . the Wisdom . . . the Light . . . the Power of the One whom you now serve."

And Dawn Bringer was no longer there.

Dancing Star went outdoors to watch the sunrise. Lifting her arms in greeting to a new day, she prayed a prayer she had been taught years ago called the Gatari:

> *You, who are the Source of All That Is,*
> *Whose loving rays illuminate the whole world,*
> *Illuminate also my heart,*
> *So that I, too, may Co-create with You.*
>
> *Blessings be to all people,*
> *Blessings be to the world,*
> *Blessings be to Thee.*
> *So be it . . . .*